THO

FROM MARS

DOWN TO EARTH

By

MICHAEL W J WILGAR

ISBN:9798552639397

.

THOUGHTS FROM MARS

Down To Earth

DEDICATION

I started to write this, my third book six months before my son Karl passed away. Since then, my world has changed, my feelings have somewhat changed, and what I think is most important to write about has also changed. The effect he had on my life was a significant influence on why I started writing and what I write. Karl Wilgar was a good boy with a kind heart with one hell of a laugh.

He, was my son.

I dedicate this book to my boy, Karl.

CONTENTS

Thoughts from Mars

Down To Earth

Introduction

Thank you for giving this, my third book the time of day. Life is precious, and so is our time here on earth, so if anyone takes time out of their life to read something I've written, I'm very grateful. My last two books were a bit of a laugh mixed in with some stuff about life. I started writing for many reasons. My children, the people in my life, the experiences I've had, because I wanted to leave a record of some sort and because a lot of chapters kept piling up in my mind until I couldn't stand the frustration anymore. I bounced out of bed one morning and started writing. Now nearly three years later, I've typed out too many words to mention and nearly drove myself utterly crazy in the process. I've been through a lot during my fifty years, probably enough to fill a couple of lifetimes. I know what it's like to feel low, I know too well what severe loss and grief can do to your heart and soul, life can be cruel. I also know what it takes to fight back, get on your feet and work hard toward a good and meaningful future.

This book is about family, life, love, loss, adventure, struggle and the stuff that makes us human. I'm sharing parts of my son's life and how he came to pass as a warning to others of how easy it is for a good soul to make bad decisions and lose their life.

The best things, the stuff that should mean the most to us, won't be bought with money. Live and learn is the only way.

Whether or not you get any inspiration from what I have to say, the truth is, the only thing that holds any of us back from living the best life we can is ourselves.

Family life and good friends are so important. Travelling around the countryside and getting into nature is a fantastic way to get fit and feel great about life and the world around us, you don't have to go far.

This is not an 'isn't life great' book. It's down to earth.

The substances that are available on the streets these days are lethal, a one-way ticket to the grave. The death toll caused by substance abuse rises every year. I lost my eldest son to drugs; his life did not have to end that way.

Michael W J Wilgar

FOREWORD

It never ceases to amaze me what you can fit into a year. When you're young, you hear your elders say things like, 'life is short' or 'we're not here for a long time, we are here for a good time.' But in those youthful years of lesser experience, it is impossible to comprehend how valid those words are. It may be the most ironic thing in the world that we must grow old before we can fully appreciate the value of our youth. 'You can't put an old head on young shoulders' is yet another one that rings the bell of truth. I suppose the reality is, many live their whole lives and never realise any of these facts. I am fifty years old, my fifty years of life experiences on this earth has led me to believe that we are here to grow, to live and to learn, ultimately to love and seek contentment by appreciating the simple things in life. A walk in the park with family, watching my kids play together, holding my wife's hand, riding my motorcycle through the countryside, reading a good book, meeting new people, meaningful conversation, and of course, a bloody good laugh. These are the sort of things I find have a higher value as I grow older. I learned a lot of what I know by listening to older folks. I try to pass on that wisdom when I find a pair of youthful ears ripe for the listening. It's very rarely instantaneous knowledge that we gain. No, it is more like a memory of things that are said to us, something our minds pick up on and perceive as useful information that could benefit us in some way in the future, so our minds store it away to be retrieved at the moment in time and place when needed. Our brain is amazing.

 Bill Bryson wonderfully describes it in his book 'The Body - A guide for occupants:

'The most extraordinary thing in the universe is inside your head. You could travel through every inch of outer space and very possibly nowhere find anything as marvellous and complex and high-functioning as the three pounds of spongy mass between your ears.'

THOUGHTS FROM MARS

CHAPTER 1

The future's not ours to see

Fifty years, living and breathing. I suppose if I could have peered into the future and seen what life would throw at me, I'd have used that wisdom to alter course and steer away from any path looking less than desirable, but, I cannot look into the future. What I can do is look to the past, the history of human life is the story of how we came to be and all the struggle and suffering our ancestors endured which enabled us to exist in the here and now. There's much to learn from history, what the experience of living brings our way, and through the choices we make.

Yes, there is much to do and lots to learn, but let's not forget, life is to enjoy. For we are not just one type of person, we are individuals with many emotions which we need as life brings changing experiences at different times. Life is many things, and it takes years of experience and learning to understand and appreciate the complexities of living a full and meaningful life. We will struggle through tough times, enjoy and love the great days. We will laugh, cry, and at times, wonder who we are and what are we doing here, it's all part of the journey.

January 2019, started pretty much like any other year, I don't make New Year's resolutions. I hope that I'll have the strength to carry me through and do the things I need to do to provide and have the best possible year for my family and myself. My eldest son Karl is always in my thoughts. Having a son who has an addictive nature, an attraction to drugs brings worries that are hard to explain. He would have been twenty-nine years old this September. Karl walked out of our family home at the age of eighteen, not wanting to live by my house rules. I know how my son felt; he thought I was holding him back from enjoying his life; he thought he knew better than me. As a father and a person who has lived and experienced much, I could see the potential dangers. I could look in his eyes and feel the direction that was drawing him in, the wrong path. Talking to him, trying to find the right words to try and reach him was a constant. The fear and frustration became so overwhelming at times I wasn't sure how I'd make it through from one day to the next.

From the age of eighteen to twenty-three, most of the time, dealing with Karl was, at times, pure hell. From picking my son up for work when he was high, picking him up from the hospital, the police station, and at times the gutter, it was crazy. I used to lie in bed at night and wonder where he was, had he eaten, would he still be alive the next morning? I had an awful feeling of powerlessness because I'd tried everything I could think of and spent money I could little afford to try and help him.

Karl reached twenty-three years old and was looking pretty awful. I'd buy him bags of food, stuff he couldn't sell to make sure he'd get something to eat. I picked him up for work one day and cried at the state of him. We talked about how long he'd been using and how the years were slipping by; he was getting nowhere in life. I offered to bring him home and help get his life sorted out. Karl was now desperate, and he readily agreed that now was the time to wise up. Within a couple of weeks of eating healthy food and training in the gym, my big son was looking better than ever. I wanted Karl to build his confidence back up, so I told him to call into the local businesses and shops to try and get a job. On his first day out job seeking, Karl came back after a few hours to tell us he'd secured employment at the local farm shop; we were all so chuffed for him, he was earning decent money. I worked out a financial plan, if he stayed with us and saved half his money, after six months, he'd be in a position to buy an apartment and have his own place. I thought that this was it, Karl was now on the right path toward a bright future.

It wasn't long until Karl started heading back up to Belfast at the weekends, I tried, but I couldn't stop him. One morning he went out to work and left some drugs on the living room floor, with his little brother and sister living here we couldn't take any risks. I helped Karl find a place to live. I told him he could still work hard, save up and get his own home. I wanted him to stick to the plan, but what I wanted for Karl and what happened next are, unfortunately, not the same thing. A few weeks later, Karl stopped going to work. He stayed up in Belfast, got wiped out and the plan went out the window. Looking back now, I think that was the opportune time during Karl's life when he could have made a fresh start and broken away from everything that held him back.

Things were rough for a while after that, no doubt, but then, when Karl was around twenty-four years old, something clicked, he started to take some control of his life, he stopped getting wiped out on drugs, got a steady job and was looking good again. As a parent, you never stop worrying, though. I'd pick him up to come home for Sunday lunch and talk to him about his past, reminding him of how bad things had gotten, there were times he could have died. The last time I brought up dangerous drugs he looked at me and said, "Dad, do you think I'd ever go back to doing stuff like that? No way Dad, no way." I loved hearing those words. I thought it was now time to get off his back and give him some space, time to forget the past and look forward to the future.

So, there I was in January 2019, looking forward to the year ahead and the challenges it will bring. One challenging adventure in particular, this year is my 'Titanic Tour', which I named this year's motorcycle trip. My good buddy and motorcycling companion, Vygantas and I planned to travel down and up the length of Britain, taking in as many sights as possible over three nights and four days on our trusty motorbikes. Last year we completed our 'Four Corners' of Ireland tour, the year before that I hit the highlands of Scotland and the famous John 'O'Groats landmark. Over the past ten years, I've been all over Ireland and the Wild Atlantic Way. Sometimes a two or three-hundred-mile day trip is enough to keep an adventuring spirit alive and well. What triggered me to get into motorcycle touring? Four simple words "What would you know?" These are the words my son said to me one day as we were driving along in my van. I was talking to Karl about staying away from dangerous stuff and bad influences. I was trying to get through to him that he needed to concentrate on his work and full-filling his apprenticeship when he said "What would you know, Dad? All you do is work." I couldn't give him much of an answer, partly because he was right. I'd got so caught up with work and building my business that the years were flying by. I hadn't got into something I always wanted to from I was a teenager, motorcycling and even more so, motorcycle touring around the country. I needed more to talk about than work, so I decided to get my licence, buy a bike and get on the road. I then started reading motorcycle adventure books which are great for inspiration. I took Karl out as a pillion passenger on some local runs, and he loved it. I bought him a motorcycle but had to sell it after a while; it wasn't enough to make him stay clean at that time. I wanted not only to feel inspired but also to be somewhat inspirational and set an example to Karl and my young children, Ruby and George. I wanted to say Dad has been there and done this and that and it is a great thing to do. I wanted to have experienced some more of the many good thing's life has to offer, so I'm able to tell my children about them, and they will know that life is good and the world is an adventurous place, after all, you can't teach what you don't know.

By Easter 2019, I knew things weren't quite right with Karl. He sounded slurry on the phone and was making excuses not to come over for Sunday lunch. I knew he'd lost the steady job he'd held down for more than two years, but I didn't know the actual reason why. When I asked him what was he on, he'd tell me he had only taken a couple of sleeping pills to help him get some sleep. I was worried about my son's future again, I dreaded the thought of him wasting his time away, so I asked if he'd like to come work for me again for a bit, if things worked out, I'd have plenty of work in the summer. Maybe this would be a good time for Karl to take the building job seriously and get stuck in. Yet again I dared to dream of him and me back working together. The week before I was heading off on my 'Titanic Tour', I brought Karl into work for a few days, I knew he wasn't right. Still, he wasn't bad either. This time was different, Karl seemed slightly out of sorts but quite talkative and open, talking about the future and what he should do. I believe he was at a junction and trying to work out what direction to go. I told him as long as good decisions were made I'd help him out in any way that I could: getting his driver's licence, getting a car, stuff like that. The day before I was off on my Titanic motorcycle tour I dropped Karl at the train station, I paid him, we hugged, he said "I love you Dad", I replied, "I love you too son". That was the last time I saw my eldest boy alive.

THOUGHTS FROM MARS

CHAPTER 2

Titanic Tour - Family man adventure

After a year of waiting and an occasional bit of planning and preparation, the 8th of May arrived. With the ferry across from Belfast to Scotland booked for the 3:30 am sailing the next morning, it was time to pull my motorbike out and get it packed up and ready for this long-awaited family man's motorcycle adventure. It is the first time since they were born, I've been away from my young children for four days and I was feeling quite nervous about it. Many thoughts go through your head when leaving the family to head off for a bit, I don't think it matters how long, it's more the fact you're breaking the routine of family life. With it being motorcycling I'm into, there is always safety to think about, mainly road conditions, awareness of what's ahead of you and what other road users are doing, thoughts of keeping yourself safe. I think the worst thing to do is dwell on it, but you certainly must not ignore the dangers. Awareness is paramount.

All that aside, excitement is undoubtedly starting to build. I'd organised my work schedule to have the day off, giving myself plenty of time to prepare the bike and everything I was bringing with me: maps;

clothes; food; tent and sleeping bag; plus, my gadgets and chargers.

My wife and I put the kids to bed on alternative nights and read them stories. With the bike ready and everything sorted, I put the kids to bed at 8:00 pm then hit the sack myself. I managed about 3 hrs sleep, stirred for a bit then got up at 1 am on Thursday.

Day 1

Vygantas and I had arranged to meet up at our starting point, the Titanic building in Belfast at 2:00 am. After a slice of toast and a couple of cups of coffee, I gave everything one last check over then quietly exited the house and hit the road. It's a strange feeling when you finally start on a challenging adventure that has been on your mind for a year. I crept up the road as I was early and no need to rush. I arrived ten minutes before meeting time, and there he was, Vygantas, also unable to sleep was extra early. I was glad to see my travel buddy again. After a hug, we snapped a few shots, made a quick vid to post on social media then rode off to the docks to catch the 3:30 am sailing to Cairnryan. Vyga managed to grab an hour or so's kip on the ship. I left him snoring away and took a dander about the deck in the dark. With it being the first sailing, there were very few people on board. When Vyga awoke, he asked if he'd been snoring, I told Vyga he'd been snoring like a foghorn and that it was a good thing too as he'd woken the Captain up just in time to avoid the boat crashing into Scotland.

With the ship getting ready to dock it was bike gear on and down to the bikes, and checked the weather. The forecast predicted heavy rain to hit this part of Scotland about now, so it was on with the waterproof gear. When the ship's drawbridge opened, I expected to see rain bouncing off the ground but was pleasantly surprised to see a dry morning outside. At least I was now prepared for anything, and anyway it was cold and breezy, the old waterproofs are also great at keeping a biting wind off the bones.

With a thumbs up from the deckhand we were off on what we knew would be the longest days ride of our four-day tour, some 600 miles, most of which would be monotonous motorway riding. We'd planned to get this part over and done with to enable us to enjoy and make memories for the next three days of our motorcycle freedom. With slightly wet roads and not much traffic about we quickened a steady pace, then, taking a right turn at a junction, I was moving up into third gear when a little fawn just over three feet tall darted out of the trees and onto a grass verge at the side of the road. It was so close I could nearly have reached out and touched it. With steam rising from its body, it ran along beside me for a few metres before disappearing back into the woods. It happened so quickly, all in a second or two. It was a welcome and warming reminder that this is a country with wildlife running around, especially at this early hour of the morning. Easy on the throttle we continued with extra vigilance along the roadside trees and bushes for creatures who have much more right to be here than we do.

We made our way through the Scottish countryside, past Gretna Green with only romantic notions for adventure and therefore no wish to elope. We kept on going until we reached the start of the M6 motorway and our first petrol stop in the land of kilts and shortbread. Although I've heard, they are also nae too bad at making a drop a whisky. Next up was the start of the monotonous motorway miles, although, between the showers, most were none too unpleasant due to the vast expanses of stunning countryside. The best of the first day's travel came near last as we branched off the M6 motorway and onto the right leg of Britain's most southern stretch of the main road, the A30. We were hampering along while being overtaken like we were sitting still by the local tarmac pilots in their two-door sports cars. Some of whom were well past their - let's put him in a home and spend his life savings date. One guy in an Mx5, just able to see over the steering wheel, passed me with a wide grin on his face at well over the ton. At a glimpse, I would guess his physical age at somewhere between 85-90, but, judging by the smile on his face, mentally he was more in the horny 25-year-old bracket. We flowed along at a speed that was of much enjoyment without risking losing our licences and wishing we'd stayed home and knitted a jumper. Leaving the very enjoyable A30, we weaved our way through a few small villages before finally making it to the lovely little escape of Lizard and our first day's destination, Lizard Point! A few photos later and a bit of stretching out, it was time to find a campsite, we'd covered some 680 miles that day and were feeling slightly worse for wear. Henry's Campsite, only a stone's throw away, was a secluded hippy style place, at only £11.50 a night, complete with free-roaming ducks it was a quacker deal. Also, on site was a cock-a-doodle-doo cockerel which Vygantas loved getting awakened by the next morning; he said it reminded him of his childhood.

We had a quick snack, and a pint in the local pub then walked back to the tents. By this point, I was so incapable of thought I auto-piloted myself into my tent while writing a quick mental reminder to never ride 680 miles in one day ever again.

Day 2

Up the next morning at 3:00 am, after a good five and a half hours uninterrupted sleep, I was wide awake in no time. Total blackout is alien to a bloke like me; I've been used to leaving the landing light on and the bedroom door ajar to keep an ear on the kids for the past ten years. Feeling good, and sufficiently revived after the day before's challenging ride, I poked around the floor of the tent for my gadgets, found my phone on the charger and opened the flashlight app. After putting on my trainers, I exited my tent and stood upright outside. Focusing through the shadows of my surroundings, I couldn't help but look up. Wow! With little light pollution in this part of the world and my eyes adjusting, I was amazed at this stunning night sky. I'd never seen anything like it. A blanket of stars, millions of them glistening with brilliance. Then whoosh, a shooting star, twenty minutes later, a second shooting star shot across the star-lit-sky, what a start to the second day.

(Staring up at the sky that morning I thought about my mother; Karl also lay heavy on my mind.)

After a light breakfast, we packed up and were back on the road just before 6:00 am. Looking at our maps we'd worked out that Vega's GPS had brought us into Lizard Point the long way around, so we worked out a shorter route to get us back onto the A30. It was a beautiful morning, riding the hundred or so miles leading back onto the M6 were very enjoyable and continued to be between the next couple of petrol stops. We were just over the halfway point to our destination that day, the Lake District in Cumbria, when we pulled in to fuel up and have a coffee break. Vyga and I talked about how beautiful it was and that we were both surprised by the vastness of countryside running the length of Britain.

Before we jumped back on our bikes to head up the road Vyga said to me, "Michael, we are so blessed with this beautiful weather", and indeed the weather forecast predicted fine weather all day. Of course, 30 seconds later back on the motorway, dark clouds swooped in, the heavens opened and it bucketed down for the next 150 miles. Oh, how Vyga laughed when I warned him later that day, "DO NOT mention the words blessed and weather for the rest of our trip". We arrived at Lake Windermere around 4:30 pm, damp, chilled to the bone and in no mood for sightseeing or for that matter setting up a tent. We took some photographs by the lake then headed up the road to secure accommodation for the night, hopefully somewhere we could get a shower, dry our gear out and grab a pint and some grub. A few miles up the road we pulled into the car park of the Swan Hotel in the picturesque village of Grasmere. After a hot shower, it was down to the beer garden out front where I ordered a burger, drank a few pints and soaked up the evening sunshine as the proverbial coachload of American tourists pulled up and loaded themselves into the hotel. Passing by with, "Oh my god Harry, isn't it just so absolutely charming Harry" comments. Half an hour later while I was on my fourth-pint, poor Harry was getting trailed down the adjacent lane by his wife who wanted to go and look at some sheep, Harry looking back at us with an expression that said, "Save me from this madwoman, I wana get drunk with you guys." Poor Harry! I wanted to cheer Harry up by shouting "Don't worry Harry, at least President Trump's back home looking after the shop" but decided to order another pint instead. Setting Harry's troubles aside, this little village of

Grasmere, once the home of the famous William Wordsworth who described Grasmere as "the loveliest spot that man hath ever found" sure is pleasing to the eye. Our hotel, a professionally run establishment, was a former coach house dating back to the 1600s, surrounded by steep hillsides it overlooks the village and lake the town is named after. It also has the most comfortable beds this side of the Mississippi. Tired and with the next day's adventuring to look forward to, we hit the sack and slept like bambinos.

Before we went to sleep that night, I spoke to Vygantas about my worries for Karl and his future. I had no idea what would unfold before the month was out.

Day 3

After a decent night's sleep in those luxurious hotel beds, Vygantas and I were in top form and on the road just before 6:00 am. A beautiful sun was shining through the morning mist as we followed the A591 winding our way through the Lake District, stopping on a couple of occasions to capture the heart-fluttering landscapes on our mobile phones. It is brilliant how good the cameras on these devices are. We branched off to take the A66 and make our way back onto the M6 motorway to get a good straight run up into Scotland and its Highlands. Reaching Scotland, we stopped for coffee and had a chat with a truck driver who was also a keen biker. Then we got our bearings to take us past Glasgow, Perth and onto the A9 that would take us to Inverness and beyond. We weren't long back on the road when we ran into a dense fog, pea soup I believe would be the right description for it. Makes me nervous riding in fog, so I hung well back following behind a Mercedes sprinter van keeping my focus on it and its brake lights, giving myself plenty of stopping distance just in case. Vygantas was doing the same behind me. For what felt like a long time, we seemed to be on a constant downhill course, the further we went down the thicker the fog became and worst of all, it got cold, freezing. I started that morning with the belief that I wouldn't require my waterproofs that day or for the rest of the trip. Now shivering and losing control of my vibrating chin I had no choice but to pull in at the next petrol station, grab a cup of coffee to warm me up and stick on my wet gear. Getting a bit wet is one thing, but shivering cold sucks the joy right out of it. Thankfully as we made our way up the A9 the fog cleared, the clouds parted and we were able to observe the charming Scottish countryside. (The last time I came up this road on my first attempt to reach John O'Groats a few years back, it rained down torrents for 360 miles until my mate Phil's bike packed in).

Riding north on the N9 I pulled over to take a picture of a vast landscape. I took off my helmet and walked back a bit to take a photo when a biker we'd passed a while back came trundling along. We hadn't seen many bikers since leaving Cairnryan on

Thursday morning. I gave him a wave and welcome smile, he waved back and pulled in behind my bike. I took a few pics then walked over for a chat. His name is John Harrison, a retired bloke just cruising the roads heading north in no particular hurry. After a bit of a talk, I asked him if he was interested in books and would he like a copy of mine, having brought some with me to hand out to anyone who tried to converse and be friendly. So, John was the receiver of my first book give away on our Titanic Tour 2019.

We made it to Inverness just before lunch so had an early one. Morale was high, pleased with ourselves at the progress we'd made that day, only 119 more miles to John o' Groats and a few more after to Dunnet Head.

With our petrol tanks brimming and food in our bellies, we headed over the Kessock Bridge which stretches over the Beauly Firth. Designed by a German fellow going by the name of Hellmut Humburg, it opened in 1982. The Kessock bridge is 1,056 meters in length and carries the A9 from Inverness over to the Black Isle and feels pretty dam impressive to ride over on a motorcycle. After 30 or so miles of weaving past slow-moving traffic and another couple more bridge crossings, it was a nice steady pace on twisty roads up to and just past the village of Helmsdale where we stopped at another unique location overlooking the North Sea. Half a dozen bikers had pulled in before us, I walked over and got talking to a couple of them. One was riding a very nice Harley Davidson which I admired for a while as they told me a bit about where they were going and stuff, really nice lads, time for another book hand out. I asked them did they read at all, they both stepped back and gave me a look up and down, I then went on to explain that I do a bit of writing and what I write about. They laughed and said, "Oh for a minute we thought you were one of those born-again Christians or something." Not quite! I gave them a book each, wished them good luck and said goodbye. I was about to put my helmet back on when I heard them saying to one of the other lads "Aye, that's him there." One of the others then walked over to me and said, "Michael? My name is Ross. I'm married to your cousin". So, deep into the Highlands of Scotland, I met a bloke who I've never met before who just happened to be married to one of my cousins. Small world moment. We laughed, took some photos together then ventured on up the road through the little town of Wick which is not as bad as it sounds.

Soon after, we arrived at John o' Groats. Not part of my original plan but Vygantas hadn't been before, and it was on his bucket list so with the sun beating down we pulled up at the famous John o' Groats signpost and took some photos. I got talking to a young couple who had not long passed their motorcycle tests and with an adventurous spirit at heart were out clocking up the miles, good on them. After a chat, I gave them a copy of my first book and headed on to that day's leading destination, Dunnet Head, the most northerly point on mainland

Britain. It was only another few miles away. Access is gained by winding your way down a single-track lane which leads to a car park beside Dunnet Head lighthouse, which sits at the edge of magnificent sea cliffs. The view is spectacular and well worth a visit. Taking more photographs of the surroundings, I realised, for not the first time on this tour, that I need to invest some money in a decent camera. Although the mobile phone cameras are excellent, when it comes to distance shots in places like Dunnet head, a decent camera would be a great advantage.

So that was it, we'd accomplished a big part of our journey and ridden down to the most southerly and up to the most northerly points on mainland Britain in good time and were feeling very pleased with having done so. What next? Well, we both thought that we could ride on for a while yet and give ourselves more time tomorrow on the west coast, an area we hadn't been before but had heard was quite impressive. Back on the bikes, we headed for Thurso, a place I stayed the last time I was up here and met a guy, Dave who lives in Thurso who'd shown me his motorcycle collection. We called to Dave's house. I wanted to give him a copy of my first book as I mentioned him in it. Thankfully Dave and his wife Fiona were at home. Fiona showed me around the back where Dave was working on his camper van project. He was getting it ready for the Ulster Grand Prix. Fiona very kindly brought us in and made us tea and sandwiches. We stayed for a short while talking, then after promising to keep in touch, we hit the road again and wound our way along some cracking wee single-track roads to the seaside village of Durness where we were able to get a couple of beds for the night in the Wild Orchard guest house, a lovely, tidy B&B, which is only a short walk away from Sango Sands Oasis, a pub restaurant just down the hill, exactly what I needed after another long day in the saddle. After eating fish and chips while admiring the beautiful view from Sango Sands restaurant I was standing at the bar ordering another pint and got talking to an Australian guy Simon. Simon asked me what I was up to, so I told him about our journey so far. I asked Simon what his story was, he then went on to say he'd rode his bicycle around the world to here and had been on the road for 26 months and fifteen days, WAOW. After telling me a bit more about himself, I got talking about writing and asked him if he'd thought of writing a book about his travels. He said no, then asked me why I started writing. I explained to Simon that the one reason I'd started writing was that I'd been researching my family tree and started to think, wouldn't it be great to find a book a great grandfather or someone way back in your family line, had written with information about what life was like for them, so, I thought, why don't I. "I never thought about it that way," said Simon. I asked him did he read much and he informed me that he loved reading. That was all I needed to hear, so up the road back to the B&B, I grabbed a copy of my book, and a Bikescarsmars.co.uk sticker then walked back down and gave them to Simon. Simon thanked me and said that after our talk he'd had a think and was seriously contemplating writing a book and when he did, he'd send me a copy. I do hope he does. I very much want to read about Simons travels. Right, back to the B&B, check all my gadgetry is charging for the next and last day's adventuring, then into another very comfy bed for a good night's kip!

Day 4

I was awake from 3:30 am, typing some notes into my tablet. I've never done this before; I usually remember as I type when I'm home. But having self-published two books, and made plenty of mistakes along the way, I thought I should take some notes of highlights and place names when I have the chance. Vygantas awoke shortly after 5:00 am and supplied a breakfast of pain au chocolate and snickers, washed down with a cup of hotel room coffee. It was good to kick start this fourth, last and hopefully, best day's touring. Fingers crossed for decent weather. With our gear packed up, we made a quiet exit to the bikes and prepared them for the journey. Back on single track roads winding our way through the hills and valleys as the sun rose in a clear blue sky, it did not take long to realise that this was going to be one spectacular experience. For the first couple of hours, we couldn't stop pulling over to the side of the road to capture the fantastic images of the surrounding landscape. No camera could genuinely capture how it feels to be standing in these places witnessing such outstanding natural beauty.

At times when I'd stopped to snap a shot, I looked back, Vyga was nowhere to be seen, I wasn't worried at all, I knew he'd be pulled in somewhere behind me capturing a fantastic view or two.

After another hundred mile or so of great roads, we pulled up at an entrance that would take us up and over the mountain pass to Applecross. Vyga noticed my front tyre was now heavily worn on one side. I later discovered my fork seal was leaking, causing more pressure to that side of my front tyre.

Riding along a narrow track with the midday sun illuminating all that lay ahead we were not prepared for what we were about to perceive. Bealach Na Ba Road is very narrow and brilliant fun on a motorcycle. Hairpin bends on the uphill climb with dramatic views lead you to the top where the sights are mind-blowing and breath-taking. Trying to process everything we'd seen so far this day was impossible. Having parked the bike up and taken my helmet off while looking with a nearly 360-degree view of the surrounding landscapes, I shouted over to the best adventure travel buddy a guy could ask for "VAGA, DO YOU BELIEVE THIS?" His answer, "No" need say no more than that, my friend.

It wasn't Everest, but it's the closest I've come to feel that I'm standing on top of the world. Even though I was in such a remote place with about 5 miles worth of fuel in the tank, I couldn't have given a shit. It was pure awesome!

From just before 6:00 am that morning, the west coast of these Highlands of Scotland just kept giving. Even Vyga, who'd ridden 4000 miles around Europe last year going to the French Alps and such places, was taken a back at what he'd seen on our adventure. Holding his arms out, he said, "Why the fuck I spend all that money going to Switzerland?" From the top of this part of the world, we headed down the twisting track on the other side which led us to the small village of Applecross where I was able to fill up with fuel at a 24hr self-service station. We had a short break, then rode back over the way we had come to admire everything once more from the opposite direction. We stopped at the next village along for a coffee break and snack. We got talking to another couple of bikers, good old Scottish lads who make a point of coming up here as often as possible. I handed out my last two books, said our good lucks and goodbyes, before mounting our bikes and heading back to Cairnryan port via Fort William, Glencoe, Loch Lomond and that damn ring road system around Glasgow, but still enjoying every mile. We got split up for a while but met again back at the ferry terminal. The only thing left to do was stand about chatting with other bikers and endure the boat journey home. Back in Belfast, we rode to the Titanic building and took some pictures to mark our journey's end. Then it was time to get our asses back home to our families, safe, sound, and with a head full of unforgettable, amazing memories from our four-day Titanic tour. Pulling back into my driveway, I checked the trip, 2,130 miles covered in four days. It wasn't the

Dakar rally, but as far as my buddy and I are concerned, it was pretty bloody close.

I planned the Titanic Tour adventure as more of a challenge than a sightseeing tour, to see how far and how many places we could get to ride through within a four-day time frame. Riding down and up the length of Great Britain, visiting the most southerly and northerly points on the mainland, then covering a good part of the famous NC 500 in the Scottish Highlands, in four days probably sounds a bit mad to most. Yes, the first day covering 680 miles was pushing the boat out a bit, it tired both of us to our limits. I won't be rushing out to do that again anytime ever. The motorway miles, some three to four hundred in heavy rain, were testing and exhausting. But the scenery, from the beautiful, and at times mind-blowingly dramatic, landscapes were beyond reward for our hardships on our Titanic motorcycle tour. Going to new places and meeting different people is a wonderfully mind-opening experience. I always think of Karl and the rest of my wee family as I ride along, I always thought that someday Karl would be right there with me, no come downs, no negative addiction possessing his mind. Me and him, enjoying the ride and loving life.

THOUGHTS FROM MARS

CHAPTER 3

This world is not good enough

Back home after the Titanic Tour, I felt a sense of accomplishment, we'd had a fantastic four-day adventure of incredible sights and beautiful weather, but as always, I was worried about where Karl would be within himself. I was straight on the phone to ask him how he was and what was he up to, he sounded tired, drowsy, but ok. He told me he'd got a part-time job in a petrol station. I told him between that and getting work with me over the summer things would be good. I told him all about our Titanic tour and the amazing things we'd experienced along the way. He said ' I'm going to get myself sorted Dad, then the next time you go, I'll go with you.'

I had no idea my son was taking powerful drugs, substances I'd never heard of or knew the effects they had on his body and mind. I'd told Karl I experimented with some soft drugs in my younger days as most people I know did, he knew I was right when I explained the adverse effects of using drugs. When a person becomes obsessed with particular substances, they'll make up ridiculous reasons for using, they waste their talents. I told him many times that my biggest worry was that he would start taking something as powerful as Heroin or similar, and he wouldn't have the strength to come off it. I thought if he ever did take something very potent that I'd have time to intervene and get him to help.

Dear God, I used to spend time thinking about what I'd do if he got addicted to Heroin. I planned in my mind building a cage in the back of my garage. I'd tie him up and keep him there until he had weaned off the drugs. The madness that goes through the mind of a parent whose beautiful child is addicted to things that can ruin their life by destroying body and mind.

We'd taken Karl for counselling sessions before, but he'd come out of them in worse form than he went in. The truth is there is not enough funding and services in Northern Ireland to deal with the addiction problems in our society.

Friday 24th May 2019, that morning I got a call from Karl's uncle to tell me Karl had been around to his grandmother's house and was in a bad way. I phoned Karl straight away; I was angry with fear for my son, how could he slip this much at the age of twenty-seven after all we've been through, Karl answered his phone, I shouted down the phone at him asking him what da hell was he playing at? I said to him, ' Karl, you are responsible for everything you put in your body. If you don't stop, you're going to do yourself damage'. At this point, I thought he was taking the sleeping pills they call blues and drinking alcohol, he sounded drunk when he said. 'I know Dad, I know, I know, I love you, Dad.' That was the last words I heard from my eldest boy.

Soft love, tough love, talking, listening, spending money, holding money back, researching and trying to find a way to reach him while attempting to provide everyday family life for my other children, the worry and stress is immense.

I'd been there so many times with Karl in the past. I wanted to go and find him, but I knew when he was in the state he was in, there'd be no talking to him, Karl was a few years older now than he was the last time he'd got himself into these states, still a boy in ways but physically Karl was now a man. I was seriously worried. I thought I'll leave it until Monday then hopefully he'd have straightened up a bit and might be able to listen to sense.

The next day, Saturday 25th May. My wife had bought us tickets for the Snow Patrol concert in our home town of Bangor for that night. We had friends round, I talked about Karl, I was back to where I was three years ago, worried and afraid for my son who is now a man. I kept thinking about all the things we'd tried in the past. That question was back in my head again, what am I going to do now? We went to the concert and listened to Snow Patrol who finished off the night doing a duet with Bono from U2. I sang along while unknown to me, my son's life was slipping away. I went to bed feeling numb and fell into a deep sleep.

4:00 am the next morning, Sunday 26th May. The doorbell rang I opened my eyes with not a shred of tiredness, instantly awake with a hollow feeling in my chest I sprang from the bed and seemed to be at the front door opening it before I even took a step. There stood a policewoman, alone. 'Mr Wilgar?' she asked. I stared into her eyes and said 'Karl'. 'Is someone with you' she replied. 'Where is he' I asked. the look of pure horror on this poor woman's face as she uttered the words 'I'm so sorry, he's dead.' It was like having a pickaxe driven through my chest into my heart, the pain I felt, and the uncontrollable noises that came from inside me can only come from a parent who has lost a child. I staggered into the kitchen, fell to my knees and shouted out ' YOU TOLD ME YOU'D NEVER DO THAT KARLY BOY, YOU PROMISED MEEE'.

After consuming drugs for quite a while, Karl's body couldn't take it anymore, his lungs gave way and filled with blood, Karl hit the ground and died within a couple of minutes, right there, lying on the floor of a council flat in East Belfast, not a soul near who loved or cared about him.

There's no describing the anguish over the following months. I cried more tears than I thought humanly possible.

I sat staring at the floor, trying to comprehend that all was lost for Karl now. I knew then that my life would never be the same again.
' *My son is dead, how can my son be dead, what an absolute disaster.'*
 After the poor policewoman left my house, I remembered something Karl had said to me; 'Dad; I want to help people with drug problems'. I decided right then I must try and do something in his name to help others like him who get caught in the drug addiction trap, the loss of Karl is such a tragic waste, he died when he was just about to start living. His life meant so much to me; I need his passing to tell something. I sent out a post on

Facebook about Karl's death due to drugs as a warning. I learned of the substances my son had been taking and sent notices out about them. Within a short space of time, many other parents, brothers and sisters of other young people who'd died the same way contacted me to tell me about their tragedies and suffering, which was a real shock and hard to take in. Once I'd realised how much of a global problem drug addiction is I decided to start the High on Life NI initiative in my son's honour. I've given talks and made videos telling of how my son got sucked into the drugs trap which robbed him and those who love him of his precious life, and also mention all the great stuff there is in the world, no need to do drugs and risk your life. What has happened can never be fixed. My son Karl is never coming back, and that is the most challenging thing for a parent to try and come to terms with, it is the ultimate disaster.

Because of the circumstances in which Karl died, and with him being so young, I wasn't allowed to go and see my son straight away. A couple of days later, I drove with my wife to the Royal Victoria Hospital in Belfast. In the morgue, a policewoman warned us that Karl's body could not be touched until after the post-mortem and the post-mortem could not be carried out until I identified my son's body,

We had to stand at one side of a glass screen while a curtain was drawn back which revealed my son lying on a bed in the same condition he'd been in on the operating table as doctors worked hard to try and bring him back to life. The laryngoscopy was still in his mouth, dry blood encrusted on his

bearded face, he looked scruffy like he used to look when he wasn't looking after himself too well.
He looked like he was asleep... 'Yes, that's my son.... that's our Karl.'
Horrific doesn't cover what it was like to stand there that day and identify my dead son; It goes against the grain of life itself and leaves scars that will never heal.

My boy Karl had so much love in him; he was a kind-hearted caring lad who had much more to experience and offer than he yet realised. My son, like so many other young people, did not deserve for his life to end this way. The first few weeks after his death, there were times I'd walk into my garage and punch myself in the fucking head for not protecting my son from the evil shit in this world. 'You're a useless bastard, what sort of a father can't protect his son' those were the thoughts that echoed through my head. If only he'd come clean and told me the truth. 'Dad, I've been taking powerful drugs and can't get off them, I'm in trouble, Dad, I need help'. I could have done something about that and he'd still be alive.

Many young people are losing their lives to drug addiction and the mental health problems they cause.
Globally, illicit drug use was responsible for just over 750,000 deaths in 2017. The number of fatalities continues to rise year on year.

When Karl started secondary school, I worried as I'm sure most parents do about bullying. One day I picked him up and asked him if everything was ok, 'I hope you're not getting any bother from any hard lads in school son' I asked. Karl replied, 'No, Dad, but the hard man in our year lifted my pencil case from my desk; I told him to give it back'. He said "What are you going to do about it if I don't?" "I told him I'd give him dirty looks, very, very dirty looks!" He laughed and gave me my pencil case back.' We drove along laughing our heads off. That was my son.

I'm not sure where I summoned the strength to carry on and do the things I did over the next few months, but eventually, it all caught up with me.

I'm strong, but not that strong.

A few months after Karl's passing, I was out early one morning cycling through the country roads close to where I live. Upon leaving home, I felt pretty good. It was a beautiful morning filled with fresh air and sunshine as I made my way down a single-track lane. I started to think as I do every day about Karl, his voice, his laugh, his unique presence. This time it was different though. The totality of the loss of my son hit me, an avalanche of emotions, my mind wild, my body shaking uncontrollably. It took me quite some time to regain myself; I knew if I didn't, I'd be in a spot of trouble. What I experienced that morning was pretty bloody horrible, a full-on breakdown, driven to a point where I lost complete control of my feelings and emotions, scary as hell. I'm not saying this or anything else to try and guilt-trip anyone into not taking the wrong path. What I'm saying is the reality of how things end up for families who lose a loved one. Everyone is an individual, once you pass into the age where you are responsible for yourself, you also carry an absolute responsibility to look after yourself, not only for you but for those who love and care about you.

Since my breakdown I've had a few counselling sessions from Cruse Bereavement; they don't take the pain away or lessen the tearful moments that come on unexpectedly, but they do help you deal with them. Never be afraid or ashamed to ask for help.

Karl had said to me that he would like to help people with drugs issues. At his funeral, friends of his came up to me and told me Karl had helped them with their drug problems.

It's now one year three months and nineteen days since I was told my son is dead. I've done many things within that time that I would never have thought of doing before. Some of those things were to try what I could in my son's name to create awareness, trying to prevent others from ending up like my precious boy. Other things I've done were to try and keep myself sane. I had my son Karl in my life on this planet for twenty-seven years, eight months and eight days. During our time I watched him come into this earth, and I can tell you it was a struggle, he had a head like an alien, but he was the most amazingly beautiful baby I'd ever seen. I changed his nappies, took him to parks, tickled him on swings, rocked him to sleep, and many other things but most of all I loved him always. During the tough times when I'd run around making sure he was eating and had a roof over his head, People would say to me 'You've done more than enough, Michael, there's no more you can do'. I never stopped searching for a way to reach him, to help him.

When a person becomes addicted to drugs, it is not only them who suffer; the difference is the addict can only see their hardship because drugs lock a person inside themselves; they fail to see the everyday struggles of everyone around them. The craving for more drugs becomes their main focus in life, time is lost, memories wasted, worst of all, they miss out on the precious moments that should be spent enjoying the company of the people who love them most, their family.

I will spend the rest of my life missing my beautiful son, Karl, it breaks my heart that he will miss out on so much good stuff that life has to offer, things that take time to appreciate. I know if Karl had another couple of years growth spared to him, he would have routed himself onto the right path and there'd have been no turning back, he was so close.

My son was not a materialistic person, never was, even at Christmas time, he never asked for much and was never overly excited about opening presents. He was good at losing things, I lost count of how many watches and mobile phones I bought him so he could keep track of time and be where he was supposed to be when he was supposed to be there, places like work and family events. It takes time to learn and respect the importance of time itself.

I placed my watch beside him in his coffin before his burial. ' You can't lose that one'.

THOUGHTS FROM MARS

CHAPTER 4

The Fatal Watch
In the year 1862,

The Ballylesson Murder/The Fatal Watch

In the year 1862, my great-great-grandfather's
brother Charles Wilgar was murdered for his pocket
watch on the towpath near Shaw's Bridge, Belfast,
by his supposed friend. Daniel Ward struck Charles
twice on the head with a stone wrapped in a
handkerchief, stole his watch then pushed him into
the River Lagan. Little did Daniel know that
Charles Wilgar had on his possession another
pocket watch belonging to his brother, Robert
Wilgar, my great-great-grandfather.
Time stopped on the hidden watch, later revealing
the moment Charles's body entered the water. One
watch marked the time of death and the stolen
timepiece found in a pawnshop a few miles from
the murder scene soon revealed an eye witness or
two. It was not long before time was up for the
wicked Daniel. Mr Ward's hanging drew a crowd of
some ten thousand or so as he became the last man
to be publicly executed outside the Crumlin Road
Gaol in the city of Belfast.
At that time, it was a huge story, not only in Ireland
and around the United Kingdom but also throughout
Europe.
Most newspapers covered the story.
In 1863 a dramatic character-revealing account of
the Ballylesson murder was published by Charles

Dickens in his journal "All the Year Round" titled "
The Fatal Watch".

Moving forward one hundred and twenty-nine
years, there I was, twenty-one years old, working on
a house, my girlfriend at the time and I were
preparing to move into in Dunraven Park, Belfast. I
was clearing some stuff from the roofspace when I
came across a little cream purse, inside the purse
was a cutting of human hair and a small newspaper
clipping. The hair on the back of my neck stood up
as I read down the newspaper article which had
been quite precisely cut out.
It read: 'About the year 1863, a murder was
committed near Shaw's Bridge, the victim being a
man named Wilgar, who was killed by a man
named Ward'...........(and so on).

What could this possibly mean? Was my find a rare
coincidence?
What are the chances?

It has been one hundred and fifty-eight years since
poor Charles had his watch stolen, and many
precious years of life robbed from him at the age of
just twenty-four.
It's been near thirty years since I found that
newspaper cutting.
 (I gave the cutting to my mother, it has only
recently turned up).
Thinking about it now, the message from the grave
could be simple reminders.

Sometimes strange things happen that are beyond
coincidence.

Two hundred and ninety-one years ago, Charles's great-great-grandfather, my six times great grandfather, along with many other people's distant ancestor's, stood on the banks of the river Rhine seeking passage to a better life after many years of persecution. They were struggling to survive in a place of starvation, disease, and brutality (the time of the mass migrations).

The struggle and suffering our ancestors endured is a reminder of how we came to be and how far we have travelled.
We have come a long way, but we still have a way to go.
No one has the right to take the life of a good person.
Wickedness, cruelty, and greed breed misery.
Our lives and the time we have are precious, spend them wisely!

With the worldwide web at our fingertips, researching our ancestral trail is a much more accessible process than ever before. Learning about our ancestors' journey is a vital part of understanding the world so we can plan and provide better tomorrows.

THIS WORLD IS NOT GOOD ENOUGH

When I think about poor, Charles Wilgar, robbed of his life at only twenty-four years young by the hand of another human being. Charles was described in the local papers at the time as a kind and mild natured person and a hard worker. Charles joined a watch club where every member paid a weekly due, so after a while, you could enter into a draw to win a watch which is how Charles acquired his timepiece before being led down a path to his untimely end. Then, one hundred and fifty-seven years later, my son Karl's death at only twenty-seven years old by drugs poisoning. I can't help but reflect on the evil, wicked selfishness of this world. My son administered drugs to himself, yes, but, these substances are made available across the globe in a world where we faulty humans live.

We all have our flaws; most of us have an addictive side; we seek something to identify ourselves as individuals. Many of us get involved in a healthy purpose like sport, travel, education, adventure etc. Like my boy Karl, some people as they search for themselves on this journey called life they get involved with things or substances that drag them off that path toward a meaningful existence and plunge them into turmoil. Many young people die because, at some point, the world made something available to them that destroyed their future. We all make mistakes. A lousy decision should not be so powerful that it can wreck a person's future, but the reality is that it can, that is why I say, this world is not good enough.... YET!

CHAPTER 5

Life is a journey

No one remembers their actual birth-day, as in, the day we were born, which is just as well, or we'd all be emotionally scarred from day one.

Not one of us asked to be born either. I certainly cannot remember sitting nowhere and shouting out, 'Hey, this is boring as shit, you, two, do that rubbing up against each other thing so I can get my ass on earth and get some living done, this place sucks!'

My earliest memories are hard to recall. I flicker through bits and pieces, playing with certain toys and riding my first bicycle but trying to remember further back is impossible. What I remember more than specific events, times or places, is feeling. I remember what innocence felt like before I learned about the big bad world and that on this earth, bad things happen to good people. It's not just as simple as the good guys are over here, and the bad over there, bad people mix in and among the good.

 Being young and trying to get through life figuring out what is right for you and what's best is quite a complicated process. These days there's much to confuse. My advice to the younger generations is never be afraid to say no when someone is trying to make you do something you don't want to do. Speak up when you are feeling confused, depressed and need some help, us older folk have been there. Most of us can spread a bit of wisdom when it comes to how you get out or move on from unpleasant feelings and horrible situations, so please ask, the right people can help you on your journey through life.

THOUGHTS FROM MARS

CHAPTER 6

The Short Life of a Much-Loved Belfast Boy

Our Karl

I was planning to sit with Karl when he reached his thirties and write a book about his life, the times we had together, the fun times he had with his mates and of course his struggle with addiction and the problems it caused my son and those who loved him. I have, however, written this book myself in memory of Karl.

In no hurry.

There I was lying on my fiancé's parents' sofa waiting on a phone call, a phone call to tell me that it was time for me to get my arse up to the hospital as my girlfriend Andrea was in labour, pregnant to the max with my baby. I was a little nervous. A couple of weeks beforehand, I was talking to a friend Alec and very proudly announced that I was a modern man and will be accompanying my fiancé during birth. 'Are you going in?' asked Alec "Of course", said I. 'OHH you don't want to be doing that Michael, do not go in for god sake, you'll never be the same again if you go in.' I was taken back by this statement from my good friend but thought he was probably winding me up, pulling my leg. Well, the phone call came around 2:00 am, and there was me at 21 years of age about to become a dad for the very first time and enter into the world of fatherhood and pure manliness. I can tell you this, after ten hours in the hell hole of a delivery suite listening to my girlfriend scream like a possessed banshee, while doctors tried to extract my son from her body using instruments I thought only existed in horror movies, I knew fair well where Alec was coming from.

In fact, I was going to have to have words with Alec. For not knocking me out with a baseball bat and chaining me up in a basement somewhere until after the birth like any decent friend would. It was pure hell on earth. I was standing beside the window, holding Andrea's hand. We were on the fourth floor. I kept looking out trying to calculate would the damage I did to my body by jumping be any worse than this living fucking nightmare. Andrea had said to me if she saw me crying she'd know something was wrong. Every time I went to slip into an emotional breakdown, she stared straight at me, so I had to bottle it up and look happy enough while inwardly falling to pieces. After what seemed like an eternity with a lot of pulling, Karl came into the world and was handed over. He looked like something that had been dumped out of an alien space ship with his big long head. It was out of shape with all the effort it took to get him out, but we were assured all was fine. He was perfect.

Looking down at Karl as I held him for the first time, only then I realised what a big responsibility a baby is and that I seriously needed to sort my shit out if I wanted to become someone who resembled a half-decent father. I handed Karl back as the doctors needed to clean him up and check him over. Having taken on board enough gas and air to fill the Hindenburg, Andrea was on cloud nine. I walked out of the delivery suite and collapsed on the floor outside where my mother-in-law Roberta scraped me up and hugged me. I was a shadow of my former cocky self but determined to give my son a good life. With Karl being the first grandchild to both sets of our parents and also the first nephew to brothers and sisters, there was no shortage of love and attention for Karl Wilgar. Everyone wanted their cuddle time and no women more so than our baby son's grandmothers. From the day Karl was born, one thing was for sure, this child was never going to be short of people who love him.

We carried our baby son out of the hospital like every new parent with no instruction manual on how to bring up this little human through all the stages of his life until the moment he was grown up and able to look after himself. How can there be such a manual considering we are all different in one way and many others? Growing up is not something that happens overnight; in fact, now at the age of fifty, I genuinely believe that growing up is endless and never fully accomplished, like many things in life.

 Karl's mother and I got together when we were very young I was nineteen and she eighteen. Looking back, I see that in the blink of an eye we had Karl, moved in together and took on family life with little experience. It was a lot to take on, and we didn't 't last as husband and wife for very long. Karl was still a baby when we split. I'm not going to go into details because there really aren't any and it was a long time ago. Divorce, no matter what is a tough thing to go through. Nobody gets married with the intentions of getting divorced unless you're a lunatic or Elizabeth Taylor. I believe us splitting up was best for Karl and us.

When Karl was a baby, I loved to take him places and show him off. I remember learning to change nappies. I would take him to friends' houses fully kitted out with baby carrier and nappy bag with all the essentials in it, including his bottle. I took Karl up to my friend Kookie's home for a visit, when I walked in with baby Karl in his little carrycot with his kit bag and changing mat over my shoulder, I think most people must have thought I was a big girl's blouse. It just wasn't such a common sight back then, but I couldn't have given a fiddler's fart what other people thought. When it was my turn to have Karl evenings during the week or weekends, it was our time, that is if my Mum wasn't hogging him. My Mum was born to be a mother. If she could have, I think she would have had ten kids. After my Mum had raised me, my brother and sisters she became a childminder so there were always kids running around our family home, that's the way Mum liked it. I love it that way too.

Back on the single scene, running around with mates, things had changed a lot in a very short time. The early nineties were not as good as the eighties as far as I'm concerned. Things were not as straight forward but Having Karl on my mind kept me grounded, most of the time. I was lucky to have him as my wee son. Taking Karl to the park where I would push him on the swing, chase him around the playground then go for walks. In the winter I'd take him to an indoor play park called Indiana Land where I'd throw him into the play ball pit then go down the slides with him on my knee. Those years go by so quickly. Karl was never a demanding child; he was easy going and was always smiling and laughing. My young son George is so like Karl at the same age, loves a good carry on, loves to laugh. Karl would sit behind me in the car laughing at something funny he'd thought off, George does the same. It brings a smile to my face every time. My Dad loved to spend time with Karl. Karl had his favourite kids tv programmes, one was called Pingu about a penguin who communicated by making honking noises. My Dad came in from work one day and said to Karl ' I want to watch the news now Karl' Karl replied 'Sure you watched the news yesterday Granda.'

That was my son.

My mother adored her first grandchild, and Karl loved her very much. Karl was deeply affected when my mother passed away from cancer; she was only fifty-nine years old. I often think that Karl may have been ok had my mother still been around, but, life is not like that.

From time to time I'd look back at myself and wish I'd done some things a bit differently, but then again none of us is perfect, and mistakes are there to look back upon and learn from. A person can't become a father at twenty-one and have the experience and maturity of a forty-year-old. I said to Karl when he was a teenager and started having problems that I wish I could have given him a better childhood more stable like the life his young brother and sister have now, he told me his problems were nothing to do with that, and I was a good Dad. He said 'You're the most respected person I know Dad' I don't know how he came up with that, but it was nice to hear.

We can expect certain things in life, but we can't plan everything that is going to happen, the experience won't allow it. We can prepare for the worst, but what happens when something so wrong happens, that it is usually unspoken.

Dear God, what I wouldn't give to hold him in my arms and tell him how much he means to me, tell him how much I love him.

With the love of family and friends, love was something my son did not lack.

CHAPTER 7

Crazy times with Karl

There are different kinds of addiction; addictive people's behaviour varies depending on their personality, environment, and what they become addicted to.

Before Karl's eighteenth birthday, I thought Karl was mainly going through the motions of being a teenager with a bit of a rebellious side. When Karl walked down the stairs on his eighteenth birthday with his bags packed, he stood in the hallway and looked in on me sitting on the sofa in the living room then said. 'Dad, I'm not living by your rules anymore, I'm moving out.' He took me by surprise, looking back now he must have planned to do this well before his birthday. I said to him 'You're eighteen now, it's your choice. I can't stop you.' He asked for a lift to his Nanny's house in Belfast, I was annoyed and said, 'No, if you want to go, you can do it under your own steam.' I thought he was making a mistake. I knew he was going to do stupid things that would not benefit his life in the slightest. I also knew he didn't want to listen to me, and he needed to learn for himself. I thought if he made his own mistakes, he'd soon realise that I was trying to look out for him and keep him on the right path.

Watching him walk out that door broke my heart. I said to him that no matter what he got up to, he needed to make sure he was there in time and in a fit state for his work in the morning. Up until this point, I knew where he was at night, living under my roof, I didn't have to worry and wonder, that all changed on my eldest son's eighteenth birthday. It's hard for me to write about as I recall the horrifying stress, sleepless nights, and many other emotional nightmares Karl's family and I went through over the following five years. Still, I feel I must write about it so it can be read and hopefully learned from.

It didn't take long for Karl to start falling by the wayside, before this he'd already messed up his apprenticeship by smoking cannabis and not caring about his future. Now I wanted him to work along with me and learn how to do home maintenance work, so at least he would have some skills to keep him going through his life. He was capable and proved it many times. It was so good when Karl and I worked together, and things were going well, sometimes months would pass with us carrying out jobs around Belfast with no bother, good times. Then the disaster started, Karl not turning up where he was supposed to be in the morning, I'd have to go around different addresses looking for him, at times I'd find him, but he'd be too far gone to bring into work. Then I'd get phone calls from his Mum or Nanny, telling me Karl was not so good. I'd go and try and talk him round, sometimes it worked, other times he was too out of it and would want to fight, I'd have to wait till he straightened up. There were times when he got angry, full of hate which was so unlike his natural self.

We all tried so many different tactics with Karl, we bought him a car and paid for driving lessons, under the condition he stayed off drugs, he promised he would, but, soon after broke that promise, and I had no choice but to sell the car. I tried the same with a motorcycle. He was a natural at riding a motorbike, but, again soon after that, he fell off the wagon, and I couldn't risk him hurting himself or someone else, so I had to get rid of the bike.

There were times when, for months, he was always under the influence of one substance or another. I talked to him about this and told him he was bound to be doing severe damage to his health. I asked him what he was taking, and he rhymed off a list of different street and prescription drugs he'd been consuming. Most of the medicines he'd mentioned I'd never heard of, I asked him why on earth would anyone want to take these drugs, what was the good in it? He couldn't give me an answer. I suppose there isn't one.

I witnessed my son in some crazy states over the years, too many to mention them all, but some stuck in my head. Karl was nineteen and he'd just been through his first sever lousy patch, his family, and I were trying to help him as best we could without funding his bad habits. I had a mountain bike which I gave him, so he had transport to get himself back and forward to the gym where he'd acquired membership. Things were going well for a while,

Karl was looking after himself, and was turning up for work.

Then he started to go downhill again, at a time that I was under a lot of pressure to get work completed on rental properties so as the owners could re-let them. I explained to Karl on several occasions that we all need to work to pay our way. Me, working for myself means, no work = no pay = no money = nothing to pay bills = financial disaster = homelessness = much sadness. I don't think this ever really registered with my son. I think he may have thought I was joking or being overly dramatic rather than stating survival facts of life here on earth.

Anyway, I was under a lot of work stress, and Karl was not right. I was driving to Belfast to get to work one Monday morning when Karl phoned me and asked 'Dad, can you take me to the hospital? I've fallen off my bike and broken my arm.' I replied 'Are you sure? You sound fine. If you had a broken arm, you'd be in agony.' Karl: 'Yep, it's broke.' I took a detour up to Karl's house and picked him up, his arm looked broken, he'd been bombing down a hill on his bicycle hit a kerb and went crashing over the handlebars.

Driving Karl to hospital, I could hardly believe he wasn't rolling about in pain, I said to him 'Whatever you are on son must be powerful.' I then told him I had to get to a job, or I'd start losing work. I told him he needed to explain to the doctors what had happened and what he had taken. I gave him money to phone me when he got sorted in the hospital, and to get a taxi home.

Around three hours later I was sitting at traffic lights in Belfast city centre when my phone rang. It was Karl, he said, 'Dad, can you take me to the hospital?' I had him on handsfree. I sat for a few seconds trying to process what he'd just asked me. Then I said 'Karl, you're at the hospital, I dropped you off there earlier,' Karl answered, 'I know Dad, I got a plaster cast on my arm then got a taxi home, but I've fallen off my bike again and broke my other arm.' I sat at the traffic lights in my van in silence, looking around me and wondering if I'd gotten out of bed that morning? Was I still in bed, and was this some crazy dream I was having? A horn beeped behind me as the lights had turned green. I snapped out of the haze I was in and drove on, asking Karl 'So you're telling me that after falling off your bike, breaking your arm, going to the hospital, getting a plaster cast fitted, that you went straight back home, got your bicycle out again, fell off and broke your other arm?'

Karl answered, 'Yeah, these things happen, Dad.' I said 'NO, NO, NO, NO. These things don't happen. These things never ever happen unless someone is entirely off their head on some crazy drugs, SON, I have work I need to get done, sort your own mess out would you?' I put the phone down and carried on with my day, if I hadn't I'd probably have ended up in a psychiatric ward strapped down to a table having my temple lobes zapped with a few hundred volts of electricity.

Unable to withstand the worry any longer, I phoned Karl that evening to find out how many pieces he was or wasn't in. After he'd come off the phone to me, he called an ambulance, telling them he'd fallen down the steps at the front of his Mum's house and couldn't move. He then went outside and lay at the bottom of the steps moaning and groaning until the ambulance picked him up and carted him off, back to the hospital for the second time that day. I talked to my boy Karl about how negative these actions of his were. It is so frustratingly agonising to watch your child throw away chance after chance at a better life, trying to find the right words that might guide them towards the right path, all the time fearing what might happen to them if they stay on the wrong road.

Karl was ok for a while then was introduced to some other mind-altering substance, mixed with alcohol, Karl turned into someone who had no resemblance to his lovely natural self. His grandmother phoned one evening to tell me Karl was going mad, jumping into her neighbour's gardens and tearing out their plants, enough was enough, we'd tried everything, soft love, tough love, and everything in-between. I could think of nothing else to do. I drove to Karl's Nanny's house walked out the back where Karl was standing pissing into a flowerbed. With the palms of my hands, I started to slap Karl around the face, shouting at him and hitting him, after a few blows, Karl was out cold. When he came around, I told him to get to bed. I would speak to him the next morning. I never hit my son, I drove home with tears flowing down my face, my heart well and truly broken, but I knew I had run out of options. If I couldn't get Karl under control, we'd lose the fight, and he'd never make it. Next morning, he came down his grandmother's stairs with his tail between his legs and genuinely sorry for his actions from the previous day. I felt that this might be a turning point for my eldest son and a broken heart was a price worth paying for his safety.

As a parent, giving up hope is never an option. Even when Karl pushed the limit of patience one morning after I told him off for coming into work high as a kite, he announced, 'Dad, I don't know why you don't understand me, I don't want to work, I just want to get high and party.' Taken aback, I replied 'Karl, do you understand that if I'd said something like that to my parents, especially my Mum, your Nanny, I'd have gotten thrashed within an inch of my life.'

My wife and I had just got into bed one Saturday night, around 10.00 pm when there was a knock at the door. That day more snow had fallen over Northern Ireland than had done for many years, roads were closed off, even main carriageways had been deemed impassable. I rushed down the stairs and opened the door. There stood two police officers, one holding Karl up under the arm. I asked what was going on. They went on to tell me that they were from Belfast, they'd received a call from an elderly lady that she'd seen someone lying down an alleyway beside a pizza shop with snow falling on them. The police called out and found Karl lying there. He'd been out with so-called friends, who'd left him there and went off home. If that woman hadn't noticed him, my son would have died that night for sure. This was another wake-up call for Karl, but, like all others, even thinking of the severity of these incidents, it wasn't long before Karl fell back off the wagon, and the Ulster hospital was back on the phone, 'Mr Wilgar, your son has been picked up by an ambulance again, he's lying here intoxicated.' I drove over to the hospital. It was around 3:00 am. I was dreading what I would find. I walked through to the back cubicles and introduced myself. One of the staffs on duty looked at me with a sullen face and then led me to the cubicle Karl was in. Muck and grass were lying all over the floor, and on the bed, he was occupying. I asked the nurse where all this mess had come from. She told me that his pockets were stuffed with it and he'd pulled it out when he was brought in. I spent time cleaning up the mess, looking around at people waiting to be seen and then at my son out of it, I felt pretty low. After I'd finished clearing up the mess I lifted Karl and took him out to my van. The fresh cold air hit Karl, and he started to come around. I looked at him, and very calmly I began to talk. I told him whoever he'd been out with had waited until he was comatose then stuffed his pockets with muck and grass sods, then left him lying in the road where he was picked up by an ambulance. I looked him in the eye and told him I loved him very much, but I couldn't do this anymore because I had his little sister and brother to think about, and this was killing me. I told him if anyone phones me again that I will no longer come running to get him. I dropped him at his grandmother's where he was living and drove away, my heart in tatters. I believe something clicked in Karl that morning, He didn't completely change, but for a long time he never got himself back into those hideous states, and he was a bit more careful who he ran around with.

We all have our struggles to deal with, should it be emotional, financial or an unhealthy addiction. Life is challenging at times; it always has been. Drugs make it so much harder. Simple tasks become impossible. Life becomes stagnant, and then they start to slip backwards. It is disastrous.

My wonderful son Karl from the moment he was born was a big part of my journey, his presence in my life was something that helped keep me steering towards the right path, the love and joy he brought gave my life more purpose than anything else could have. From cuddling him as a baby to holding his little hands as he sat on my shoulders as a toddler while I walked through the park. His grandparents fussing over him with him being the firstborn grandchild, his laugh, his smile, and the love he spread are things that can never be forgotten or replaced. I'm grateful to have had my boy Karl

Wilgar in my life, and I will spend the rest of my life not only missing him but also trying to be a man he'd have been proud of. If love could have saved my son, he would have lived forever. Life is precious, and so is the people we spend our time with.

THOUGHTS FROM MARS

CHAPTER 8

Gett'n high – addiction

Ok, let me start by saying there is no such thing as a recreational drug. There are recreational activities, which will make a person feel good, no drugs required. You can try and cheat putting any effort into feeling good by popping a pill, sniffing a line, or going the whole hog and injecting a poisonous substance into your bloodstream. But ultimately you will pay for this through the withdrawal effects your mind and body will go through, pure hell I believe. No one has ever looked back and said with any degree of honesty, 'I'm delighted I took those drugs, they have left me with such fond memories'. The truth is drugs are a living nightmare for the user and all those who love them.

Addiction?

Addiction is a hard thing to explain. So many of us have an addiction to something useful like a sport or activity that is healthy. I think we all need something to fill the space in our head and keep us focused, something so we can say to ourselves, I am me, and this is what I like to do, this is my thing, and it is part of who I am.

There are so many positive things in life that we can get involved in that can enrich our lives and make us feel good. When a person gets involved in street drugs, especially at a young age when the brain is going through crucial development, the consequences are beyond disastrous. For me as Karl's father, witnessing the path he took and the many other opportunities he could have grabbed hold of at different stages during his short life. The chances he had to make something of himself and live a good life are evident. Still, his addictive side got him trapped in the world of street drugs, and that alone stopped him from developing into the man he could and should have been. How many other young men and women have ended up like my son, trapped/enslaved in destructive addiction that keeps them from all the wonderful things that life has to offer? My boy was one of 189 souls that lost their lives to drugs in Northern Ireland during 2019 alone. That doesn't include the many driven to suicide over the effects that street drugs have had on them. Then there are the many thousands wandering around wiped out, not knowing what's going on most of the time. Every day people lose their jobs, their home, their family and friends because the decision to try street drugs led them to become addicted to something that took everything good in life away from them, robbing them of themselves and destroyed their life.

It is frightening to think that something you can purchase then consume can have such a life-altering destructive effect on the way your life will turn out, but the truth is those substances do exist, the grave I visit with my son's name on the headstone proves it.

There is no sense, no logic, no reason for anyone's life to end up this way. The receptors in the human brain are amazing things, when you mess with them you mess your life up, it is that simple.

The only sure way for it not to happen to you is not go there in the first place. Leave street drugs well alone and get yourself a hobby. Should it be hiking over mountains, swimming in the sea or riding the roads of our beautiful country on a bicycle/motorbike/car or public transport etc., There is something positively life-enriching for everyone.

I write about this because I want to tell my eldest son Karl's story to try and help others make the right choices in life. I want the world to be a safe and healthy place for not only my children but for everyone else's as well. It has to be this way.

 My son did not want to die, but he was unable to make the right choices in life because of his addiction to street drugs. He could have so quickly gotten addicted to something positive and meaningful, but those decisions my son made led him to his premature departure. I know Karl was not fully aware of the consequences of his actions, no matter how many warnings he was given he never thought it would be him, but it was, and he paid the price, so have I and the rest of his family and friends. I know in my heart that if Karl could come and talk to me now for just a minute, and believe me, I have wished for such a moment so many times, Karl would say, 'I'm sorry Dad, I didn't mean to cause so much hurt'. I don't wish for his apology.

Karl is on my mind before I open my eyes every morning, and he is there when I close my eyes at night. I only wish I could hold my firstborn son in my arms, look into his eyes, and say ' I love you son' and hear those words, the most magnificent words a father can hear from his child ' I love you, Dad'.

The line between positive and negative can be very narrow. The wrong choice can take a person over that line in an instant and alter their future dramatically. No one can live another person's life for them, to make the right decisions you need to be honest with yourself and choose wisely, because, if you kid yourself and make the wrong choice, the only person you are lying to is yourself, but it is you plus everyone who loves you that suffers.

I will miss my eldest son for my forever. Karl was a huge part of my life for so long, from a new born baby to lad, who was on his way to becoming a man. I had many hopes for our future as father and son, imaging us working side by side and going on adventures together. I had so much more to talk about, so much more to teach him and he would teach me, as our children do as they get older. I guess Karl is still teaching me stuff as I learn more from the thought of him. One thing is for sure, and that is I feel Karl in my heart and remember him in my mind, there is not a person or a substance on Earth or anywhere else for that matter that can rob him from me in this way. I will carry Karl with me, wherever I travel should it be for work or pleasure,

Karl Wilgar is and always will be my son no matter what. He was a good boy with a kind heart who got caught in a trap.

People, family and friends have asked me how I feel, am I ok, well, to be honest, I never really know exactly. What I do know is I'll never be the same again, what does that mean? For months I didn't know the answer to that question either, but now, I do. I have always had struggles in my life, as I'm sure most, if not all of us do. There were times though, brief times when work was going well, I'd plenty of work in the books, and Karl was doing well, things were moving forward, and everything seemed right in the world, I felt that all was as it should be. I will never feel that way again, but, I won't allow that fact to burden my life, especially when it comes to my family.

No one sets out to destroy their life and purposely hurt those who love them.

Previous generations of my family, and other people I've known have suffered from addiction and or mental health issues.

Things like addiction and depression used to be swept under the carpet to supposedly save a family from disgrace and embarrassment. This primitive way of thinking is thankfully changing. We are now starting to open up, talking and understanding more. This means we can now start to really focus on tackling the problems and help people who suffer from these horribly destructive illnesses. There is much to be said and done!

They say that things always get worse before they get better. In the world of addiction and mental health issues it's very much the time for things to get better, hopefully a lot better!

CHAPTER 9

This is life

What is the meaning of life? Some people make the meaning of life question sound all deep and mysterious like a quest which should be delved into with heightened awareness, something that could only possibly be solved by those few exceptional humans who possess incalculable intelligence. Which, all sounds both confusing, unbearably boring, and is of course, total bollox!
Something as simple as helping an older person cross the street, saying something nice to someone to cheer them up, loving someone and spending time showing it. These are just some of the meaningful things which give exceptional purpose to existence.

While writing, and doing a bit of questioning about my existence as a side-line, I started to do some research into my family tree, which I wrote about in my second book. I feel that in doing that research and finding out a little about my ancestors, I gained quite a lot.
Understanding the journey and struggle for those who lived before our time, and the road which led to our existence, I find that stuff mind-blowingly fascinating. Learning that hardship is part of life, that struggle is not a punishment dished out to those of us who deserve it. The pain of living is part of the human condition and has been from the beginning of the human race. The way we feel when

we are trying to work out a better idea of doing something. Trying to solve problems to ease the discomforts in living can become overwhelming at times, but, they are the same emotions that our ancestors felt in their search for a better way to live. The struggle is a driving force that pushes us forward so we can reach out and grab hold of our better tomorrows. Without this driving force, we become stagnant, and if we are not doing what our instincts are telling us to do, we get depressed, confused, we feel bad about ourselves and the world around us because we start to believe that things will never get better. We may even think that life will continue to get worse for us forever.

Feeling weakened and cynical about life can take hold of a person and become hard to shake free from, this is when wisdom passed down, learned through conversation or reading can help a person make good decisions (we must listen, we need to feel and act appropriately).

My experiences in life have taught me that feeling down is a signal that I need to adjust. Taking time out to sit back and analyse myself can reveal much about certain things. I can then make slight changes, which may also involve taking better care of my physical and mental health. They are both linked, so by working on the body, we are also looking after the mind and vice-versa. Tablets/drugs might numb unwanted feelings within us, but they can create a confused and emotionally complicated mindset, they'll never be a cure (nature is the most excellent cure).

We can have many negative stories and images thrust in our direction these days, it is easy to get distracted and forget ourselves, the good people we want to be, and the positive life we want to live. The beauty of life is not in the complexities of modern-day living, but instead in simplistic family values, appreciating the world around us, and being kind to one another. Doing what's best to build a healthier world for our children, our descendants and ourselves, for me, is the meaning of life. Continuing to grow through learning and looking after our physical and mental wellbeing keeps us healthy and robust, it is a constant throughout life. Doing what is right for your body and mind is the foundation to build and live an enjoyable and meaningful existence.

All of what I've said here and, in the past, particularly the year since my beautiful boy Karl passed away has been to try and create awareness about how easy it is to take the wrong path and head in a negative direction. Dangers which, can lead a person to ruin or possibly end their tomorrows. I want what we all want, a safe and healthy world for our children.

Taking drugs was something my son did, not who he truly was. I watched him grow from a new-born baby to a fun-loving child and a loveable, talented, but sometimes troubled young man. Karl was unique in his humour, his laughter, right down to the very essence of his being. I've shared parts of Karl's life and how it ended. It is what Karl would have wanted me to do. He was a loving, caring young lad.
It's been over a year since my first son passed away, it's now time for me to let go, so he can wholly rest

in peace, and now Karl can do so knowing his story has helped other people who suffer/suffered as he did.

I'd have given my life to save my son's, but life does not allow us those choices. Reality is our choice, our creation and that which we can work with and build upon.

The battle for a safer, healthier world where people can concentrate on positive growth without harmful distraction is a constant fight. Part of responsibility and purpose in our lifetime is to take action that will help our descendants live a better life than we have.

Words are all-powerful; they can lift you high or crash a person to their knees. Trying to work out what to say at the appropriate time and expressed with meaningful emotion is one of life's most significant and most pressing challenges. Learning through experience to understand and control our emotions so we can be aware and express with realistic intention what we want to say and do, is the gateway toward actions that will lead to creating a better, safer, healthier world.

I'm well aware that growing old and learning about life is a privilege denied to many. Time is limited. None of us has forever to figure out what we want from and also donate to life.

Live your life, love and respect yourself, and appreciate every day as much as you can. Love this planet, it is our home, it's worth is beyond words.

The more we love and understand the natural world around us, the more we will do what's needed to preserve it.

The greatest thing you can spend on yourself and those you love is meaningful TIME!

CHAPTER 10

Being Dad

Or more to the point, being a parent, without doubt, the most challenging job in the world. Trying to work out what's best to say and do for your child is a stressful thing in this world of turmoil — trying to be strict enough to teach discipline without turning into the worlds grumpiest git and also being as loving as possible without becoming a pushover. It is both testing and unbelievably rewarding. It is also the thing I love most: Being Dad!

Unfortunately, not every child gets loving, caring parents to raise them, that doesn't mean they can't go on to be wonderful parents themselves; many people have done precisely that.

My children = My everything

Karl's little sister and brother, Ruby and George.

Our Ruby is something else. Twelve years old now and not long started into her first year in a big school. Ruby's strength of character and artistic talents radiate from her little soul like there's no tomorrow. My daughter is, and has been from she learned to string sentences together, the bossiest person I've ever met. Ruby likes to tell me off if I come home from work with a cut or a scrape, she also likes to order me about for no particular reason other than she feels I very much need it, she may have a point.

Our George will be ten years old very soon, he loves a good carry on, and a play fight just like his big brother used to when he was a young boy. Both he and Ruby are frequent readers, George has taken a keen interest in writing, recently he's started his own diary journal, noting down his daily goings-on around the home and family trips. I find my children's growth and development to be the most unique and vastly important aspect of my life, nothing means more to me than my kids, and I am well aware when the time comes for me to part this world Ruby, George and Karl will consume my every thought.

We must do all we can to secure a safe and stable environment for all the children of this world; it is no less than they deserve.

George last Easter:

"Dad, we have to give up something for forty days, and forty nights, so, I'm giving up chicken because it's not fair on chickens. What are you going to give up Dad?"

Me:

"Ok son, let me think......... lamb, I'll give up lamb, George."

George:

"That's good, Dad because that's not fair on Llamas."

That is my wee son, he's so like his big brother.

CHAPTER 11

Inspiration and adventure

I suppose all adventures big or small start from some form of inspiration, whether it begins with watching something on TV or picking up a book and reading about someone else's adventuring experience. It only takes a split second to start the thought process off in a direction that will lead a person to their next adventure. I started with a motorbike and a couple of small tours, then, watching Ewan McGregor and Charlie Borman doing their epic adventures and reading their books. I read, watched then thought, yes, I want some of that. What I have done so far is minor league compared to what a lot of guys have done and written about. I am not in competition with epic adventurers or anyone else for that matter. My writing is a mixed bag of memoirs to amuse, my love of family life, and motorcycle and other adventures. I do things that are realistically feasible for more or less anyone. All it takes is a bit of inspiration and planning. The great outdoors is ours to enjoy. I believe the more we get out and enjoy nature and our surroundings, the more we will think about ways to look after and preserve it. My writing is about the adventure of life, past, and present, good and bad, plus some real and made up funny stuff, I think.

I've heard people say 'life is crap' and yes, fair enough, I know as well as anyone how dire things can get but if you keep thinking life sucks, guess what, your life will surely suck. There is much good around us and plentiful enjoyable things to get involved with. We need to look in the right places!

CHAPTER 12

Good Old County Down and the East Coast

Adventures on the doorstep

We are blessed to live in a country of natural beauty that does not suffer the natural disasters that so much of the rest of the world has thrust upon them. Long spells of rain and the strong gusts of wind is hardly much to complain about. Okay, the politics is a sham, who could sort out that mess? For the vast majority, the troubles of the past do not define us as people. Let's not bring up religion. It's far too dull. We can learn from history and live for today, working together for a better future and while we are at it, let's genuinely enjoy this great country and the things it has to offer.

Where I live in County Down, I only have to ride a few miles along the shoreline of Strangford Lough to take in the beautiful, breath-taking scenery. Strangford Lough is the largest inlet in the British Isles, covering 150km. Leaving the town of Newtownards driving along the east side of the lough towards the village of Greyabbey, you will come to Mount Stewart, a 19th century house and gardens built for the Marquess of Londonderry. Now owned and run by the National Trust, it is a stunning place to visit. The views across the lough from the car park on a sunny day are good enough reason to pop in. Should it be for historical information or to roam the grounds and have a picnic, it is one of my wife and I's favourite places to go and visit. Being members of the National Trust for many years, we like to support and take time out to enjoy National trust properties whenever we can. The Trust do a top-class job of preserving these old places for our and future generations. Head on out the road another couple of miles, and you will come to the quaint little village of Greyabbey which has some excellent attractions. First, its Abbey ruins dating back to the 12th century, it's well worth a visit if you're interested in that part of history. I love walking around the graveyards in these old places and reading the headstones, some fascinating ones in Greyabbey. However, it is heart-breaking to see how many children did not make it to their 10th birthday because of the harsh conditions of those days. Tough times, these days it's hard to imagine. Makes me feel very grateful to be living and bringing up my Family in the relative comfort of this modern era. Other things Greyabbey has to offer are many antique shops if you're up to grabbing yourself an old bargain or two. There are also a few excellent cafe restaurants for choice.

This coastal route is lovely and the road twisty, so, if you do decide to visit, take your time and be careful, especially on a motorcycle. It's a take it easy and appreciate the scenery road, not a, let's push my riding skills to the limit place. Further, on out and after passing through another couple of small villages, you will come to Portaferry, where, you can either follow the coast road on round and head back up the East side of the Ards peninsula, driving through many more villages. Portavogie, Ballyhalbert, Ballywalter, with the view's over the Irish Sea. On a clear day, you can see parts of the Scottish coastline.

Further along, you will come to Millisle and the Ballycopeland Windmill, the only remaining working windmill in East Down. Next along the east coast is Donaghadee, a great place to grab a bite to eat and a pint of Guinness. Then we are back to my home town of Bangor just 12 miles from Belfast city centre.

Back to Portaferry where you will find the Exploris Aquarium an exciting place to visit. The Aquarium has all the usual attractions but is also a rescue centre for lost or injured seal pups that have turned up around the lough or Ards Peninsula coastline. The second option of travel at Portaferry is the ferry over to Strangford, which carries vehicles and their passengers across some of the strongest currents you will in a ferry crossing but never fear, these ferryboat captains know what they are doing and give a smooth sailing onto the Strangford slipway. If you are into your fish dishes then The Lobsterpot restaurant in Strangford would be the place to head to.

A couple of miles up the road from Strangford to the right is Castle Ward, another 18th-century property owned by the National Trust with vast grounds and lough shore walks it is another favourite place of ours to visit a few times a year. Castle Ward is also where they filmed parts of 'Game of Thrones' the historic farmyard is the location of Winterfell. It's also where you will find the Whispering Wood and other scenes including Robb Stark's Camp. With 36km of trails for walkers and cyclists, Castle Ward is a top destination to visit here in Northern Ireland.

Downpatrick is about another 7 miles up the road. Just before Downpatrick, there is a road to the right which will take you down the other side of Strangford Lough, past Delamount, a great place to go for a family fun day or scenic walks. You can see some of the islands that are dotted up and down Strangford Lough from Delamount. As you travel around Strangford Lough, each point gives a different view with its unique beauty. Further along and into the village of Killyleagh, the hometown of Hans Sloane, The creator of milk chocolate. There's an excellent food and chocolate festival held here every year to celebrate the village's most famous son.

Another lovely little town and to complete the lap of Strangford Lough, you're into Comber just 2 miles from Newtownards where we started. Comber square has some excellent pub/restaurants and cafes and is situated about 8 miles from Belfast city centre.

Back-up into the town of Downpatrick, the Cathedral there is said to be the burial place of Saint

Patrick. You can visit the Saint Patrick visitor's centre for information or head up the hill to the Down County Museum and find out some fascinating stuff about local history.

Heading in a southerly direction along the coast you will come to Dundrum Bay and the award-winning Blue Flag Tyrella Beach. A flat sandy beach 2 kilometres long and backed up by dunes it is a lovely place to visit and relax on a beautiful day.

The next town on this side of the country a little further along is Newcastle County Down which lies at the foot of the Mourne Mountains and close by Tollymore Forest Park. Slieve Donard is one of many mountains in this part of County Down and the tallest in Northern Ireland. I have been on 20-mile charity hikes up and around the mountains of Mourne, and spent the next few days after, with a permanent grin on my face, having the vision of what I witnessed still fresh in mind, the sort of views that makes a person feel very humble and blessed at the same time.

Well, that is just a snapshot of some of the beautiful things to go and see here on our doorstep in Northern Ireland. I've only scratched the surface.

I wonder what's down there? - motorcycle adventure.

Had a great day out on the Triumph Tiger, I didn't go very far, but, I went to many places I hadn't been before. Off the beaten track so to speak, little roads I've noticed many times with the family in the car and often thought 'I wonder what's down there?' So, today was the first part of my "I wonder what's down there, Tour!" I love the sort of roads I rode on today, twisty and bumpy in many places, great fun at a steady pace. If you're a middle-aged guy who's doing the whole mid-life crisis bit, just bought himself his first big boy bike, rushed out and bought an R1 with matching latest Power Rangers outfit? These are not the roads for you, unless? You want to end up on the history channel. Now, I'm not slagging off middle-aged men having a mid-life crisis, Dear me, I like to try and squeeze at least three in a year. Although I fear I'm fast approaching the age when I will not be able to use the mid-life crisis excuse anymore, I'll just be a stupid aul ballix!

Well, according to the experts Beast from The East two, Beast from The East one's second cousin, is making it's a way to the UK and Ireland so there may not be too many more trips for a while. One hundred and four delightful miles covered, well worth getting geared up in long johns and thermal-lined Gore-Tex. Sexy as sponge bob square pants I tell yee!

LIFE

We can concentrate so much on what's happening tomorrow that we forget to live today. When we remember to live, life is good!

People and Places

When out travelling around different places, what I look forward to and enjoy as much, if not more than the areas I'm visiting on my adventures, is the people I meet. Should it be another biker I've bumped into while filling up at a petrol station or someone that has stopped as I'm taking a photo and admiring a particular view. It never ceases to amaze me where a Hello there can lead to when it comes to the art of communication with another soul.

CHAPTER 13

Motorcycle day trips - Get out of town!

Slieve League

It's Friday 22nd February 2019, this time of year my motorbike is usually tucked away undercover in the garage. Still, with the weather being so mild for February, and with a long list of places to go and visit, my old buddy Kookie, aka Paul, and I set off early morning for Slieve League in County Donegal. It is situated around 50 miles or so west of Donegal Town. Slieve League is a mountain on the Atlantic Coast and forms part of the Wild Atlantic Way that stretches the full length on the west side of Ireland. The Wild Atlantic Way has many fantastic places worth seeing. Slieve League was on my list as a doable day trip.

I left home in Bangor, County Down at 6:45 am and rode over to a friend Paul's house in Dundonald, about 6 miles away. Then the both of us hit the road and weaved our way through a bit of early morning traffic before entering the M1 motorway and heading west for Enniskillen in County Fermanagh. It wasn't raining, but it was a chilly damp morning with thick grey cloud blanketing the sky, leaving the road surface moist, shouting out at me 'NO HARD BRAKING, I'M SLIPPY AS FECK!'. "Yes,

I know, LOOK, I'm keeping my distance," said I back to the road.

After passing through some little, blink, and you'll miss them, villages we arrived at Enniskillen then headed up the left side of Lower Lough Erne. A slightly longer way than going on the right side of the lough, but it is a much better biking road with less tree coverage so more chance of a bit of dry tarmac. It was still a bit damp in places, but good. We stopped to fuel up just before Ballyshannon. Paul took off his helmet to reveal a shivering worried-looking soul. I asked 'You cold mate?' to which Paul replied, 'I've been cold since Lisburn.' He'd put on his racing leathers over thermals thinking that the leathers would be warmer than thermally lined Gore-Tex, the like of which I was wearing and very toasty warm in. A lesson learned the hard way for ma wee buddy.

After fuelling up, we headed for Donegal Town then up the coastal road to Killybegs and on through to Slieve League, the lanes getting that bit narrower and hilly along the way. However, the tarmac is in pretty good order for somewhere so rural. We arrived at a car park where a gate closed the narrow laneway which leads you on up to Slieve League, so we parked up, had a well-deserved lunch break and prepared ourselves for the hike up the hill. Then something beautiful happened, other people arrived, opened the gate, then closed it and drove on up the laneway to the top. Brilliant!

So, we packed up, did the opening and closing of the gate which we discovered was to keep cattle in, then rode on up the hill to be greeted by some of the most mind-blowing sites I've seen in Ireland. Now, my vocabulary isn't what you would call extensive in any way shape or form, but even if I were the king of wordsmiths, I still don't think I would be able to put the impression that a place like this makes on a person into words. Slieve League and its surroundings are both humbling and awe-inspiring.

After taking some pictures and having a chat with a Canadian guy, it was time to hit the road as the wind was blowing a gale and my terrific friend was turning a most unattractive shade of blue. Luckily, after only a few miles and back closer to sea level, the clouds parted, and the sun spread much-needed warming hellos over the world, making my travelling companion a much happier chap by far.

Riding on dried out roads it was time to take full advantage of grippier tarmac, so we headed back the way we came, very much enjoying the twisty stuff back to Enniskillen for a visit to my favourite butchers on the planet: O'Doherty's. Black bacon, streaky bacon, black pudding, white pudding and an excellent selection from their varied range of burgers. When my belly is happy, I'm happy. I do love my food.

After another coffee and a chat to a lady biker standing by our motorcycles, we hit the black stuff and homeward bound we went. I pulled into my drive around 3:40 pm, around 9 hours after I'd left that morning with 349.5 miles on the trip. My friend Paul and I had a great day. It is quite something that can fit into a day with just a little planning, and a willingness to go for it.

Donegal before we die from boredom!

Usually, by this time of year I've ramped up a few hundred miles at least on my motorcycle, but with the travel restrictions that were put in place late in March this year as part of the COVID 19 lockdown, it just hasn't been possible to get out and about much. With restrictions starting to lift, I decided that it was time to hit the road and get a day adventuring done and dusted. During the week, I contacted my good travel buddy, Vyga to see if he was up for heading out on the bikes, and as I'd predicted, my mate was more than ready to ride.

Looking over my long list of places to go before I snuff it, I was looking for somewhere that would be easy to stick to the social distancing rules. Donegal was the top choice, many countryside and coastline miles away from other folks. The only place we'd have to go was service stations to fill up our petrol tanks, with keeping our helmets on as masks, and rubber gloves packed for handling the petrol pumps I was happy that I'd taken all precautions necessary for a safe journey.

After such a long wait and with me recently purchasing a new bike the Kawasaki ZZR 1400, It's a great feeling to have a trip planned and ready to go. Even if it's only for a day, travelling to somewhere new and taking in impressive scenery can lift the spirits and refresh the mind as nothing else can.

With Vyga living near Cookstown and I living in Bangor Count Down, we decided to meet up in the village of Augher, situated in County Tyrone, it lies on the route to Donegal and has been used by us as a meeting and stopping point in the past.

As usual, my hyperactive mind and energetic soul of excitement had me up at 3:00 am. With lunch and other bits and bobs packed on the bike, and breakfast including a couple of coffees onboard in my belly, I text Vyga to let him know I was leaving then hit the road as quietly as possible so as not to wake the neighbours (hopefully).

Darkness was starting to lift as I made my way past Belfast and onto the M1 motorway. With a more or less straight run to Augher, the riding was comfortable as the sun started to rise in a blue sky with the odd cloud hovering here and there, all looking peachy for a good day ahead.

After meeting up with Vyga, we headed up the road leading west through County Fermanagh, up the left side of lough Erne and into Donegal. With the sky now clear blue and the heat rising we entered the N56 and rode along until we reached the port village of Killybegs, famous for its massive fishing fleet, the first sense you get from the place is the smell. This fishy scent enters the nose about two miles before your eyes get a glimpse of the area. With its vast array of fishing boats and ships, some as large as you'll see anywhere on the planet, Killybegs is well worth a visit. Trundling along the R263 at the village of Carrick, we turned right onto the L1225. Riding through the stunning countryside along smooth single-track roads, with plenty of twists and turns, these are delightful places to ride along on a motorcycle. I was slightly concerned about how the big Kawasaki would handle on roads such as these. But honestly, that machine feels better on any road than any bike I've ever owned and I've held a lot of different motorcycles in my time. Another right onto the R230, we made our way across to Adara, and the Glengesh Pass. Yet another breathtakingly beautiful spot in this land of unlimited visual pleasantries.

The R230 lead us back onto the N56, with its near-perfect surface and sweeping bends you'd think this road was designed for motorcyclists by motorcyclists. After many enjoyable miles passing through some gorgeous villages, we stopped at a siding on the coast road in the seaside resort of Dunfanaghy. While parked up at the side of the road, drinking a coffee and looking out over the Atlantic Ocean, our presence was appreciated by the locals who tooted their horns and waved as they drove past. The Irish people of the Wild Atlantic Way are about as warm and welcoming people as you'll find anywhere on the planet. With it being such a beautiful day, at the end of the N56 approaching Letterkenny, we decided to head up the road to upper Donegal and ride along a route known as the Inishowen 100. With more twists and turns than the Monaco Grand Prix circuit, these single-track roads need negotiating with an air of caution. Especially nearing Malin Head, Ireland's most northerly point, as this is rural riding and the trails become quite bumpy with the odd hairpin bend thrown in for good measure. After a stop off at Malin Head, it was time to head for home. Pulling back into my drive at around 3:00 pm after covering 426 miles from early morning, what a day, motorcycling along excellent roads with world-class scenery on display, what a great way to spend a sunny Saturday.

The Wicklow Mountains

Saturday, 20th June 2020 and this time it was up early as usual and on the road heading south for County Wicklow and the Wicklow mountains.

I'd taken the family down to County Wicklow to a little cottage for an Easter break a couple of years back and fell in love with the place. Wicklow is only 30 miles or so on the Southside of Dublin and can be easily accessed from the M50 Motorway. I met up with Vyga at the Castlebellingham apple green services on the M1 motorway at 5:30 am. We rode for Dublin took the M50 and got off at the junction for Glendalough. Glendalough is a stunning place with streams, lakes and mountain views it's the perfect place for a visit with family and friends. We were early birds, so with everything closed in Glendalough, we headed up into the mountains through the Glendasan valley and stopped at the Lead mines to take in the stunning views and take some pictures. After a coffee break at the Blessington Lakes, we spent the next couple of hours riding around the mountains through Sally's Gap and over to Johnnie Fox's the famous Irish pub, known as the highest pub in Ireland it's well worth a visit if only to take a few momentum photos. Another beautiful day of sunny weather after the forecast was for dense cloud, we can't believe our luck sometimes when we're on these trips. Heading back home and just over the border into Newry and Northern Ireland, I went one way, and Vyga rode the other. After spending a couple of hours on lovely twisty roads with stunning scenery on display, the hum of the motorway very quickly becomes monotonous. A slip road off the motorway at the far side of Newry called to me so off I turned and rode home via the Mountains of Mourne, Castlewellan, Downpatrick and Strangford lough. Back home with another successful Saturday's 400 miles adventuring completed, I was knackered, ready for a hot bath and a cold beer.

THOUGHTS FROM MARS

CHAPTER 14

Good judge of character

How many times have you heard someone say, 'I'm a good judge of character ya know'. A self-confession that usually comes from someone who's recent history would suggest otherwise. I think the truth is that we are all growing steadily, some people learning faster than others, some give up the ghost on the whole learning thing and think they already know everything they need to, the sort of person who has lots to say about things they know very little to nothing about. There are some brilliant people out there no doubt, but no one knows it all, and no one ever will, that is a pretty good thing indeed. The excitement of knowing there is always something new to learn is undoubtedly a driving force on its own. It is an individual's personal choice if they want to learn about a particular subject or not. As we grow older, we can identify these differences between each other, they become more transparent, and these are the times when we make our individual choices whether we want to spend time with certain people that have been in our lives. Maybe a friendship/relationship becomes stale, and it's just not worth hanging onto. No matter what the history is, sometimes going separate ways in is the smart thing to do. I don't think anyone needs to be a good or bad judge of character; it's just life and life is about learning. Only a stubborn fool refuses to learn from experience. Life will always throw up something new we can learn.

Learning and moving on is something that we need to do so we can grow and live a better life, a good life; it's normal to not get along with everyone.

THOUGHTS FROM MARS

CHAPTER 15

There's no stopping the clock!

And neither there is, from the beginning of time, before the first tick tock clock had even been invented, the unstoppable force of time has always been there. From the moment we are born to the day we part this great earth, it marks our moment in history as it did for our forefathers and will do for all those who come after us. Quite a miracle when you take time out and think about it. It's easy to get caught up in the quick pace of modern living and not take time out. It is vital to make time to celebrate life and living by doing adventurous things, exploring the great outdoors, appreciating our surroundings and enjoying the company of our loved ones in these generally peaceful times we live in. Sometimes we have to look back to give us the right direction to move forward. It's good to learn about the history of Northern Ireland and Ireland and the fact that for many hundreds of years going back, those who lived before us did not have it so lucky, they did not have the freedom and the comfortable living conditions we enjoy to be able to go exploring and adventuring. Many complain about trivial stuff. But the truth is we are now living in the best times there has ever been here. So, why not make the most of it. Go to places you have never been before and see things that will open your mind to the great outdoors and all it has to offer; it is quite remarkable. The clock never stops ticking, why not start planning for your next adventure now?

CHAPTER 16

GOD - possibly maybe

Do any of us have an identical set of beliefs or
believe in God or spirituality in the same context? I
know there are bible thumpers out there who would
bore the living daylights out of you, check out
BIBLE BASHER on google, the description is not
good. Then there's the atheists putting down on
Christians, a lot of whom happen to do a lot of good
for others. I think there is an acceptable truth
somewhere in the midst of it all, but we really do
need to stop with the persecuting. Putting down
other human beings to make yourself feel superior
and them feel inferior is a pure awful thing to do.
I don't think of God as some all-powerful super-
being who looks down on us from up above and
will someday either let us into heaven or send us to
burn in hell (that stuff happens right here on earth).
I don't believe that any more than I believe in Santa
Claus, but then again, I think about and love the
idea of Santa Claus, so maybe that is what God is?
God is the essence of Santa Claus, so, therefore,
God is not only Santa Claus, God is Santa Claus
and Spiderman, God, is Superman and Ironman,
Captain America, Batman and Robin, Cat Woman
and Wonder Woman. God is Thor, God is the
Avengers, Conan the Barbarian and the X-men.
God is the Guardians of the Galaxy, Rocky Balboa,
the Ghostbusters and Mary Poppins. GOD is the
hero within us all. God is all that is good and right

in this world. God is the truth that sets us free and allows us to be the best that we can be. God is love, life, and the meaning of life is growth, to grow and learn, learn to do the things that can make this world a better place. God is watching a child being born. God is standing at a grave, reading the inscription and knowing your world was a better place when that person was still alive. God is wanting to help someone in need and doing something about it. God is the story of my son's life and the message he has left behind. Life is precious, don't waste it!

I'm not telling anyone this is the way it is and you have to believe me. I'm just a middle-aged family man, a builder from Belfast that's been through some serious shit in his life. I never asked for most of the shit that happened in my life, and I'm pretty sure most people who have been through some serious hard times ever asked for it either, but it happens. No matter what religious beliefs a person has or has not, if a human being is a good person who lives a good life and tries to help others then no one has a right to judge them or put them down. If those people who seem to take great pleasure in the persecution of others concentrated on looking after their own life, the world would be a much better place. AMEN!

There are lots of people on this earth, believers and non-believers none of which I have any intention on spending eternity with and I'm sure there's quite a few can say the same about me. I do not care, and neither should you!

GOD

Sitting on a bench in a beautiful place with your eyes closed after a long winter feeling the sun's rays warm your body and soul, aye, that'll do me rightly!

Chapter 17

What love is

It's mmm yeah. A whole lot of things that take time and experience to work out. Love is getting up in the morning when you're still tired and kicking your ass into work so you can provide for those you love. Telling someone something nice to try and make them feel better because you sense they need it. Noticing someone struggle then lending a hand. Watching your children laugh and smile and saying thank you, even if you have no idea whom you're saying thank you too. Yeah, I guess that's love. Giving something up so you can be a better you for not only yourself but all those who love you. Telling someone something they need to listen to rather than what they want to hear. Realising that even the simplest good thing is something worth doing. Knowing that the sort of person you are matters much more than how much material wealth you have. Love is everything good. Love is all the things that will make this world a better place for future generations.

Love is something we very much need.

THOUGHTS FROM MARS

Chapter 18

Down to earth

This planet is our home, so far, in and around 107 billion humans have ever lived here. There are now 7.8 billion people living on earth, give or take, I'm not sure. So, that means 99.2 billion people have passed away since we first came to be, 200 thousand years ago. The earth itself is a ball of elements that's around 4.5 billion years old, give or take a few million weeks or whatever. The diameter of our universe, the Milky Way, is estimated to be 93 billion light-years across, 558 trillion miles and is estimated to be somewhere close to 13 and a half billion years old. All the above is a bit much for my simple brain to consider. The fact that when I go on a plane on holiday and fly at an altitude of 30 thousand feet, is quite the thrill. Taking into consideration that when we're up there above the clouds at 30 thousand feet, there is a mountain top that stands a little over 29 thousand feet, Mount Everest, which quite a few adventurous folks with strong legs and much stronger will have climbed then straddled the peak, is quite the mind boggler.

When I think about the incredibly impressive humans that have worked out calculations to the scale of the unimaginable, it makes my head spin. Even more so, I hasten to consider as well, those amazing humans who devote their life to medicine, doctors who perform life-saving surgery on other human beings, Superheroes! If I got asked to perform surgery on someone, I couldn't do it. The person requiring surgery would probably end up having to pick me up of the floor because I'd fainted at the thought of it. If you want your house fixed up, I'm your man. If you need your body fixed, it's a big NO from me. If everyone were like me, we'd all be living in a hut beside a swamp.

Surrounded by mind-blowing happenings every day, life here on earth is a miracle in itself. Struggle, hardship, and catastrophes happen all the time also. How we deal with life stuff ultimately predicts who we will become and what sort of life we will live. There is always much to learn. Keeping ourselves grounded, DOWN TO EARTH, I believe, is the best way to live!

We are like a home; we require good foundations, a strong structure and regular maintenance if we are to withstand everything the world will throw at us. Looking after yourself is the foundation of your life.

THOUGHTS FROM MARS

CHAPTER 19

Thoughts from Mars

Why thoughts from Mars? Well, it's pretty straight forward really. I'm using the men are from Mars and women are from Venus terminology to point out that I'm a bloke, so, therefore, most things I write about are from an ordinary man's point of view through my experiences of life on earth. Then again is there such a thing as ordinary when it comes to describing us, humans? After all, 7.8 billion people are living here, and no two of us are the same, so considering those figures, to describe any humans as ordinary has no factual accuracy. Which is great, it means learning about and appreciating our differences will keep us entertained for many years to come. We will be less likely to turn into robots and bore each other to oblivion — writing a letter to the president of the USA begging him to press the big red button because we can't stand the monotony.

This brings me to my 196th reason for writing and probably one of the most interesting ones. I am leaving a diary for my descendants.

I sometimes think about the possibility of one or some of my descendants in maybe 100/500/1000 years or so researching their family tree as I have done, and coming across my books on some digitalised historical database and then reading them. Perhaps they will be on a space ship zooming past Mars on a mission to search for new worlds. Will they then start to write a journal about their life? If you are that person reading this book and I am long gone, I want you to know that while I'm sitting here writing this book, I am thinking of you. I hope you have a good life and I need you to know that I love the thought of you, so, therefore, I love you.

P.S. Although I am long gone, maybe you could write me. Thoughts from Mars!

Hello, Thoughts from Mars, this is Shooting Star. My name is Ashford Wilgar, the year is 2898, I'm onboard the space ship Shooting Star approximately 34 million miles from earth, just past Mars, and we are on an adventure!.............

THOUGHTS FROM MARS

Chapter 20

Remembering Karl

In the morning, I open my eyes, he is the first thing on my mind. I remember in abundance the uniqueness of my son. Carrying him as a baby, how his hand felt in mine when he was a small boy, how he laughed when I tickled him on the swings and chased him around the play park. How he talked and his laugh, no one else on the planet sounded like him, how he looked smelt and felt when we hugged are the things that made my son unique. I would love to be able to hold Karl in my arms again, I have thought about it so many times since he died. To sit with my firstborn and look into his eyes and tell him how class he is, tell him how much he means to me. We went through so much together, and we talked a lot when he was alive. I told him every time I saw him that I loved him. I have so much more I wanted to talk about with Karl and so much more love to give him. I have thought about the things I did say to Karl, and many other things I could have said, somethings I would have said had I had more time, had we been spared the time to grow and learn together. It takes a lifetime to fit all the important things in because it takes a lifetime to understand them. I could write a would have, should have wish list a mile long, but that wish list is an impossible one. I have and continue to learn much from Karl passing away, I'd be the world's biggest fool not to. The pain from losing my son is beyond horrendous, it is beyond words. There's no getting over losing a child, all you can do is learn to carry the weight of the pain, work through the bad days and appreciate the not so bad. All this sounds pretty heart-breaking, but the truth is some people go through a lot worse. I'm lucky to have what I have. I have a loving wife, and an amazing daughter and son, if I lose sight of that then I have learnt nothing and really am not very wise at all.

Imagining, I guess this is the hardest part to let go off. From the moment our children are born, I suppose most parents start to have preconceptions, brief thoughts about what the world will be like and what our kids will be doing in that world when they are older. Most of all, I think that when they are young children, we wish for their health and happiness. I never pushed Karl towards the building trade, I wanted him to make his own choice, and if that were doing something else he'd be happy at then, I would support him. When Karl left school, I asked him if he wanted to work for me or try something different. He said he wanted to work for me and start training as an apprentice joiner. It made perfect sense at the time as I'd built my business up over the previous years, things were going well, and it was the ideal time to take on a young lad, everything seemed to fit. It would have been brilliant if things had worked out. Through the heartache, I remember Karl with so much fondness.

Some days are ok, and others are tough, just like most other peoples. Writing this book has been tough. I hope it might find its way into the hands of people who may need a jolt in the right direction, maybe even help someone decide to choose the love of family life and or adventurous undertakings rather than the negative draw of drug addiction or other life-destroying temptations. I feel that Karl has pushed me to write this book, helping others, as he wanted to do from, beyond the grave. The boy had my head turned for sure, but, he was bloody brilliant.

That was my son.

Some days I look across to the passenger seat of my van and visualise him sitting there beside me the way it used to be, like it should be. Life goes on!

One day when Karl was around ten years old, I picked him up in my Dad's van, we were driving down the road when dark clouds suddenly rolled over the sky, a couple of minutes later lighting flashed and thunder shook the air around us. I looked around at Karl in the passenger seat, starring out the windscreen with his eyes wide and mouth a gape he asked 'Is everything going to be ok, Dad?' It was the first time my wee son had seen such a spectacle. 'Everything's going to be fine son; it's only thunder and lightning' I answered. He calmed straight away.

That was my son.

SUMMER SON

From that morning I was told

that my eldest son no longer lives

I have searched through heart and soul

for answers to the questions. I ask myself

Why did my boy consume the poison that he did?

Was it to escape the pain, that he kept so well hid?

Pain is part of living it's in the mind and heart

we can overcome it if we draw the proper chart

If we try to escape our struggles through substance abuse,

the pain becomes amplified and our minds even more confused.

Life can become unbearable, hardship every day

your mind is trying to tell you that you have lost your way.

It's time to change direction, head toward a better day.

Listen to those who genuinely love you, they will know the way, for they have suffered too on their journey to this day.

Talk and talk, then talk some more about the things that lay heavy on your mind.

You will unravel the twisted passageways of the things that have made you blind.

Blind to the great things in this world, like family, friends and love,

these simple things the most beautiful blessings, sent from spirits up above.

Like sitting in the summer sun loving everything that blends, that overpowering feeling and the hurt it can mend. The blending of the heart and mind bringing goodness to your soul,

all the beautiful things in life that help make you feel whole.

My son's body was destroyed by poisons that exist.

But the memory of this beautiful boy will stay with us in this final twist.

For he loved life and living, he got confused and lost his way.

The wrong decision with that confusion led him to his final day.

So, the message from him through me to you I'll say it now today, life is precious, don't take risks and throw it all away.

For life upon this earth is a blessing to embrace.

Every one of us is a part of this life that makes up the human race.

My son did not discriminate about religious or cultural beliefs or whether straight or gay. Those thoughts quite simply never entered his mind. Everyone could be his friend without being judged.

Yes, my son made mistakes, the biggest of all cost him his life. But he was a good boy with a kind heart. I will think of him every day for the rest of my life.

On days of clear skies while resting somewhere, anywhere, I feel the suns radiating heat warm my body, and I think of my boy.

I'm just a Dad who lost a son.

THOUGHTS FROM MARS

Chapter 21

Write all about it!

If you are feeling a bit low, maybe a bit lost or possibly stuck in an unhealthy addiction. An excellent way to get a bit of focus is to write about your life. It doesn't matter where or what part of your time you start to write. You could maybe do what I did and jump in the here and now then branch out from there. I think once you get into it, you'll begin to understand yourself, life and the whole decision-making process more than you could ever have imagined. Whether you share those writings with anyone is up to you; you are in control, it's your life.

I want to try and encourage anyone who has been through the horrendous struggle of addiction and made it out the other side to a good and meaningful life to consider sharing your story; it could be someone else's survival guide. Through talking sharing and caring, we can all play a part in helping people who very much need it.

THE PEN IS MIGHTIER THAN THE SWORD!

These days its more

THE KEYBOARD IS MIGHTIER THAN THE GUN!

highonlifeni.com

Chapter 22

You matter!

I remember being young, from those teenage years up into my twenties and early thirties, was challenging and somewhat confusing at times. I feel it is essential to live your life and experience as many good things as possible. The message I try to get out there is: life has much to offer, seek and ye shall find, so to speak. The depressive, 'what's the point' attitude sucks so many people in, life's too short to listen to that.

If you have an unhealthy addiction during those younger years, yes, that is time wasted, you can't build a good life with a negative outlook, but you can if you acknowledge the error of your ways, change it. How many of us have headed down the pub to have a couple of beers then ended up drinking way too much, waking up the next day with deep regret because the day ahead is going to be a struggle instead of enjoying as previously planned? With drug addiction, this ends up with every morning becoming a waking nightmare, unable to prepare for the future because your mind is locked in turmoil from the intoxication of substance abuse. A person can start to change their life around in an instant. Many people reach a point in their life and realise that the drug-infested life they've been living has been a waste of precious time. The smart ones seek help, learn what they need to move forward into a life of meaningful existence, and live to tell the tale.

Those who don't learn, die young, and that's about as sad as it gets.

I wish it were my son Karl sitting here telling his story of how he survived, helping others to break free and live a good life, that is what he wanted to do. It was in Karl's nature to care; he wanted so much to stick around. My son told me he wanted to make it up to his little sister and brother for the years he'd spent wasted, and he told me he wanted to help people, that is why I'm trying to help in his name. My eldest boy was a skip and a jump away from the right path. Karl now lives on in my heart and memory, encouraging me to do what's right, and help if I can. We can all play a part in building a better world, no matter how insignificant. All good deeds are essential.

Please, look after yourself out there. Live a good life. YOU MATTER!

CHAPTER 23

Our Rosie rabbit

Rosie Rabbit (I had to give her a mention; she was part of our family).

06/10/2020

For nearly eight years now, Rosie, our wee pet Dutch breed rabbit, has had the full run of our garden as well as her hutch which has a tunnel leading into her insulated winter burrow. Until four years ago we had two rabbits, the other one was Flopsy, a lop-eared English breed rabbit who passed away at the age of five while we were on holiday, it was a sad time for our children, but now with Rosie gone too, our garden will never be the same. Our children Ruby and George are devastated that Rosie has passed, they both spent time grooming and talking too Rosie, at the age, they are they'd hardly remember the garden without rabbits running around in it. My wife and I are both very saddened as Carissa was the one who fed and watered Rosie. Every morning and evening, when my wife let Teddy our dog out, Rosie would come running to the back door to get her rabbit biscuit. I look out into our garden now, and my heart sinks. After spending every morning over these past years seeing Rosie there, watching her run around the garden using chairs and plant pots as an obstacle course. In the afternoon I'd take her out carrot cuttings while preparing the diner and she'd usually be waiting in the same place by her hutch for me to bring her this daily treat. I said to my kids we have to be grateful that we had Rosie and Flopsy our pet rabbits in our lives, and that they had a great life running free in the Wilgar family garden. It is ROSIE'S GARDEN!

CHAPTER 24

The right path / The right outlook

No matter who you are, what you look like or how much money you have in the bank, we all have our flaws. Getting onto the right path and staying there is made easier when you have the right outlook, stay positive. The fact is there is much good going on around the globe which unfortunately does not get the attention it deserves. There are many reforestation and rewilding programmes underway. Millions of trees have been and are being planted; wildlife is being reintroduced into areas around the UK and Ireland. Renewable energy is the fastest-growing sector, globally. As the need for clean, sustainable energy increases and renewable technologies get ever more advanced, more and more projects are being developed in more significant sizes and complexities. Improvements in agricultural technologies and production practices have significantly lowered the use of energy and water. In short, people care about the earth and are taking more responsibility for the planet that will be inherited by our children. There is much work to do as always, but it's not all Mr Doom and Mrs Gloom. Don't get sucked into the soul-crushing vortex of despair, get involved and help out, even if it's just forking out a couple of quid a month to a reforestation programme, every little bit helps toward a better world.

CHAPTER 25

A few quid in the tail

I'm a worker, since way before leaving school I was well aware that if I wanted to have a good life, I'd have to work hard to pay for it. I left school over 34 years ago in which time I've spent most of those year's grafting hard, so I have a few quid in my tail pocket to pay for a roof over my family's head, put food on the table and live a comfortable life. The past lot of years I've been able to head off on the odd motorcycle adventure around the UK and Ireland, which I love. I'm so appreciative for the memories both my family life and my escapades have brought me. It takes hard work and making the right choices to live a good life, and that is a good thing, indeed. My mum used to say 'If you get something for nothing, it means nothing to you'. The right path might be a hard one to stay on, at times you might veer off in a less desirable direction, I know I have, but the longer you keep yourself routed on the right road, the better you'll get at it. There are many things in life to get involved with that enriches life and the world around us. Sport, Adventure, Reading, Writing, Education, Charity projects, the list goes on. If you want to get involved in something but you're not sure what, I'd advise some healthy research on the internet, I'm sure you'll find things that will inspire you.

THOUGHTS FROM MARS

A life worth living is a life well lived.

We all love a good laugh but life isn't a comedy show, treat it like a joke and it will do the same back. The real fun in life is doing stuff that you'll want to remember with people you truly care about and who genuinely care about you.

I like to push myself to take on a challenge now and then. I wish I'd done more when I was much younger, but I'm thankful that I started reading and doing adventurous things when I did. The truth is, anyone can do it and it's never too late.

If you want to learn more about the world and the people in it, read books, not articles.

I hold my heart in my hands and look out at the world. I see family and friends. I know the value in simple things like a loaf of bread and a warm hello. I know what it is to love and be loved, and I realise that there is no greater blessing than life.

Bless you and your loved ones!

AUTHORS NOTE

Writing this book has been challenging to say the least. The affect my son's death has had on me plus the many people who made contact, friends and strangers who shared their grief and offered their love and support, has played a large part in why I have written this book. What I've written is not only the story of my son's passing and the impact it's had on our family. This book reflects the devastating grief that many families around the world suffer after losing a precious family member to addiction. I've shared the parts of Karl's life I felt are relevant in telling how and why he died, how easy it is for a good person to make a fatal mistake and how important it is to grab the right opportunities when they present themselves. We are human, and as human beings, we have our faults.

If you need help, then please ask for it. If you see someone struggling, please reach out to them. There are addiction services and mental health support groups who can help people get on the right path, the first step may be hard, but it's a positive move in the right direction. One good decision can change a life for the better for the rest of their life.

This book is dedicated to my son, but it is also in honour of those who have suffered, as we, Karl's family, have suffered.

We are united in our loss and in our love of family!

Karl Wilgar 18/09/1991 – 26/05/2019

A much-loved Belfast boy

Michael W J Wilgar.

Other books by Michael W J Wilgar

BIKES CARS AND THOUGHTS FROM MARS 1

AN ADVENTURE BOOK LIKE NO OTHER

BIKES CARS AND THOUGHTS FROM MARS 2

BORN IN BELFAST

MICHAEL'S BOOK RECOMMENDATIONS

THE BODY-A guide for occupants

By Bill Bryson

GREAT THINKERS

By The school of life

INTO THE WILD & INTO THIN AIR

2 books By Jon Krakauer

JUPITER'S TRAVELS

By Ted Simon

IN CLANCY'S BOOTS

By Geoff Hill

GOING THE WRONG WAY

By Chris Donaldson

APOCALYSPE NEVER

By Michael Shellenberger

A HISTORY OF IRELAND

By Jonathan Bardon

DO THE BIRDS STILL SING IN HELL

By Horace Greasley

RETURN OF THE DAMBUSTERS

By John Nichol

SAS ROGUE HEROES

By Ben Macintyre

THE TATTOOIST OF AUSCHWITZ

By Heather Morris

THE SHOE MAKER AND HIS DAUGHTER

By Conor O'Clery

A MAN CALLED OVE

By Fredrick Backman

Look after yourself out there.

THE END!

P.S. People don't dance enough these days!

Printed in Great Britain
by Amazon

50799501R00075